# * THE ONE MINUTE INTERVIEW *
## by Richard Ciavarelli

Dedicated to Anna

I0404118

**Forward by Larry Wilson**
"There's only sixty minutes in an hour. This book will save you 10% of that in time, effort, and lost opportunity for the rest of your life. It's the best investment for building up your confidence, being better prepared, and improving your interviewing skills. Read It!"

**Larry Wilson**
President & Founder of Wilson Learning & Pecos River Learning. He is a member of the Speakers Hall of Fame and has published several books, including "Play to Win! Choosing Growth Over Fear in Work and Life." He also worked with Spencer Johnson to write the "One Minute Salesperson" as part of Johnson's "One Minute" series of business books.

*A recent International Poll was taken specifically designed for retirees, the Question asked was, "what do you regret most in Life?" The answers varied from relational to personal to professional, but the number one answer that stood out above the rest at 55% of the replies was: "not pursuing my dream job"!*

# INTRODUCTION

*Shakespeare wrote*, "All the world's a stage, and all the men and women merely players; They have their exits and their entrances, and one man in his time plays many parts" Most of us in our lifetime will have a job and in today's society it is perfectly normal to have more than one career in ones' lifetime as we also balance our families and other responsibilities. Therefore, "The One Minute Interview" is for everyone! Whether your new to the market place, or a victim of corporate downsizing or deregulation or merger, laid-off, presently unemployed, seeking a better career to improve your life for yourself and your family, or simply desiring to increase your interviewing and general business skill set – this book is for you!

The One Minute Interview is more than a thumbnail sketch yet less than a dissertation, rather it's a handy Reference Guide that you can take anywhere to easily refer to at anytime, even to offer last minute tips and confidence booster while awaiting the Interviewer! It approach's the job search holistically from your last or present job, through the transition period and search, to after landing that desired role. This book includes methodologies from leading experts in the field, multiple job service reference guides, various charts and checklists, exercises, articles and quotations, and a free copy of my Work Search Log to get you started.

It is my hope that in using the "The One Minute Interview" you'll be more equipped and confident to aid you in your quest for a successful work-search in today's marketplace. From hereafter, I will refer to "The One Minute Interview" by using its acronym "TOMI" (for convenience sake). Finally, in order to completely learn how to apply the principles in this book to its full potential, it may of additional help to re-read each chapter before moving on to the next one. Remember, you only get one chance to make a first impression! Make it a good one!

let's get started! ...

# **CONTENTS**

Chapter  **I**     **What Not To Do**

Chapter  **II**    **Preparation**

Chapter  **III**   **The Resume -** *Plus*

Chapter  **IV**    **The Interview**

Chapter  **V**     **Skill-Set Building Exercises**

Chapter  **VI**    **Career Counselor**

Chapter  **VII**   **Reference Guide & Resources**

# THE ONE MINUTE INTERVIEW

*There once there was a man who had a difficult childhood, less than one year of formal schooling, he failed in business more than once, initially defeated for the legislature, having his first fiancé die on him, defeated for speaker and elector, was the only son who lived past 18, defeated for the Congress and Senate twice, and even defeated for the Vice-Presidency. But at age 50, on November 6, 1860 he was elected the 16th President of the United States. If you guessed Abraham Lincoln, you were right! A man who overcame incredible odds and persevered until he achieved the highest most respected, and most powerful political position in the world. The point here is - he never gave up, and neither should you! Winston Churchill, the great European orator and statesman once gave a simple yet powerful fourteen–word speech that went "never give up, never give up, never give up, never – never – never – never – never! So, if you are currently seeing employment or causally searching for a better career, don't give up' until you find the Company/Career that is what you want and deserve.*

*In this day and age the competition is fierce, and since job security is a thing of the past, it is in ones' best interest to be as prepared as possible at any given time. Throughout this book I will advise you on every stage of the job search in its entirety, as well as a complete job reference guide, exercises and checklists to utilize as preparation for the actual Interview. To begin, it is equally important to be aware of areas that may inadvertently negate or prolong the chances of getting that desired role. The following are some potential characteristics or weaknesses that may be transparent to others -- but not to you.*

# CHAPTER I

## WHAT NOT TO DO

*First of all,*

**Don't Stress**

There is a man who was once fired by Henry Ford II, who in his autobiography said, "I thought, 'look, if it can happen to the best, it can happen to anyone – you're not alone," he says. That man is none other than Lee Iacocca, who didn't turn out so bad after all. Remember you are starting over again, as in all things finding a new job takes time -- especially one in which meets all your standards regardless of your qualifications. Experts indicate that regardless of experience or education it could take up to six months to secure new employment. Be patient and brace yourself for what you're up against such as the economy, the competition, and timing. Truly believe that you have an ability which somewhere-someone-someplace is in need of. Have the confidence in yourself that sooner or later you will secure a role, or find one temporarily until that desired one opens up.

**Don't forget to re-adjust your budget**

Consumer credit experts suggest that it's very important that you revisit your budget immediately, because statistics show that most families are just two months away from financial disaster. In determining your expenses, separate the needs and basic essentials from the desires. Food and shelter should be the priority, and you know what you can do without during this time-frame. Make a list of what income you have coming in during the next few months combined with your present savings. Compare your findings with a list of expenses and possible unforeseen incidentals, and see where you are financially. Many people prefer not to bother with budgeting and ignore their situations incurring a deeper debt. However, it will be to your advantage to take seriously what's happening and do away with all the unnecessary services and expenses until you return to full time work. Ross Perot stated, "brains and wits will win ten times out of ten over capital spending" – my point is use common sense. Talk to your creditors before it gets too late in the game, and be sure to use your credit cards wisely. If you need to, make use if community provided services wherever possible. However, if you need further assistance, you can call the Consumer Credit Counseling Services at (800) 547-0099.

### *Don't be dishonest with yourself*

Get alone somewhere away from your everyday routine to reflect and re-evaluate what has taken place in your life, and where you stand. Take a sheet of paper and divide it down the middle with columns labeled "Pro's" – "Con's". Self-appraisal is neither easy, brief, nor inspiring, but most importantly it needs to be honest. Set apart some quality time to access your strengths and weaknesses. In order to help determine blind spots or short-comings, you may wish to seek out the opinions of others for additional insights. If you slight the truth, it will only prolong your opportunity to grow or maintain a professional stature in the future. Reappraise the opinions offered by former employers and friends, there is at least a 50% chance they are right to some degree. J.F.K. said, "an error doesn't become a mistake until you refuse to correct it".

### *Don't neglect family and friends*

Some people may have the tendency to ignore the support from those who care about them the most, especially when a difficult time arises. Include these people around you in your thoughts, feelings, and plans. You may benefit in more ways than one. Don't allow embarrassment to enter into your emotions nor reject their counsel, because they may be the avenue that eventually leads to securing your new role. Statistics indicate that a large percentage of jobs are acquired this way -- welcome their help and counsel. However, nobody wants to hear sour grapes, which has the tendency to creep its way into your attitude or conversation and eventually into the interview.

### Don't lose focus

Nitche said, even the strongest have moments of fatigue. If presently unemployed, keep in mind that you have a job -- that is finding a job. Unless you're a seasoned specialist (e.g., as in medicine), cast a wide net to include occupations that are similar in nature and function, or former ones. Develop a strategy to pursue companies and fields congruent with your level of exposure, even if it means traveling farther or perhaps relocating. Stop at nothing in getting the word out that you're available, be persistent, and act upon every lead that comes your way. Back in college we had a saying that went, "The main thing is to keep the main thing -- the main thing."  And the main thing here is to get a job.

### Don't be dishonest

Abraham Lincoln once commenting on honesty said, "When you tell the truth, you only have to remember half of what you say". Never -- ever lie, nor stretch the truth out of proportion during your interview, or on your resume. Be sure to be above-board especially on an application because it's considered a legal document that can be, and usually gets verified. If there is a section that requires information regarding an undesirable issue in the past, be honest. Remember, there is never a need to defend yourself because if you're in the right -- your right and the truth will surface eventually. But if you're in the wrong, you have no defense either. Admit where things went wrong, and redirect that portion of the conversation on what you have learned from the incident. If questioned about anything, be specific and discuss it openly and how it made a positive effect in your life. Focus on the problem and not the person(s) involved; be careful and separate personalities from performance. On the other hand, don't spill your guts either. Don't offer more than what surfaces because it could backfire and breed unnecessary insecurities on both ends

## *Don't settle for less*

Vince Lombardi said, "Winning isn't a sometime thing. You don't win once and a while, you don't do a thing right once and while, you do them right all the time. There is no room for second place – there's only one place – and that's first place". It's not uncommon to receive several offers right away, but the chances of making a big mistake rise in the hastier of a decision that you made. Avoid accepting roles less than your qualifications because you could get labeled a less than desirable title, and hinder future possibilities more than you think. Everyone deserves a respectable salary for an honest day's work; so don't be afraid to ask for what others are receiving for the same position. If you're unsure as to what the salary range a particular company would be willing to pay, you can check around with other companies in the field and get a general idea first. Later on in the book, I will address this issue in detail, as well as "what to ask" for and how to get it. One should be capable of performing their job well and enjoy it -- after all, ones' occupation consumes a major portion of the day and is practically ones' life. Remember, the highest reward for your efforts is not what you get for it, but what you become by it.

# STEPS IF LET GO FROM A JOB

1. <u>Be Professional</u>
   Show some style in your turning over projects and in your exit interview. Take the higher road here and try not to show your anger towards anyone nor ruin the chances of returning to the company or getting a referral. You can use all the friends you can, and may be able to help out someone else too.

2. <u>Take advantage of any Company offered out-placement and training</u>
   Some companies offer networking groups, ongoing education and optional classes You should make every opportunity to utilize and get involved in everything as you will need to stay sharp for future interviews and in an effort to be prepared.

3. <u>Be Flexible</u>
   Be willing to entertain other fields than you have been accustomed to in the past. Take this time to learn and build up your strengths and to even expand them. Keep in mind even if you do get same job with another company several things may be different and various skills may have needed to be performed.

4. <u>Stay in Shape</u>
   Because you will not be initially as active as you were while on the job, it is important that you keep several factors in mind. Be sure to get your rest and plenty of sleep. Also, eat healthy and get your exercise. Emotional support is also important for your self-confidence so seek to make time friends and family.

5. <u>Be Social</u>
   The key here is remembering to stay active as it will be to easy to get too laid back waiting for the phone to ring. Go out on every interview you can, go to seminars and job fairs, hang out with business

associates. Losing your job is stressful, knowing that and being around others will lessen the effect. Be certain to get out of the house frequently and be social – as interpersonal skills are always being tested on the job!

6. <u>Broaden Your Search</u>
It's always more convenient to focus within the area of your current physical location, however if one method is not generating your preferred position expand by seeking new websites, or recruiters, reaching out to friends and contacts you have not been in communication with until you succeed.

7. <u>Be Willing to Relocate</u>

   There may be extenuating circumstances that make it impossible for you to move but that said due to your current local economy or demand for your current line-of-work may leave you no alternative to stretch the area(s) – start with locations you are familiar with then expand accordingly.

# THE ONE MINUTE INTERVIEW CHAPTER ONE REVIEW

## "What Not To Do"

Don't panic

Don't forget to re-adjust your budget

Don't be dishonest with yourself

Don't neglect family and friends

Don't lose focus

Don't be dishonest

Don't settle for less

Steps if let go from a job

# THE ONE MINUTE INTERVIEW
## CHAPTER II

## PREPARATION AND SEARCH

*In his legendary book "How to win friends and influence people", Dale Carnegie tells the story of a job hunter who spent several days gathering as much information as possible about a prospect company and the interviewer as he could --which he then used this information to his advantage. He even went as far as standing out in front of the building for an hour to interact with the people coming in and out and take some general observations. The interviewer was so impressed that the man had taken the time and interest- that he hired him on the spot. Obviously, this won't happen in every case, but it might in yours. Moreover, it certainly will be to your advantage to gather as much information as possible anyway, if not for the great impression you will make, but also to determine if you really want to work there. You can gather information about an intended employer through a variety of venues. Start with co-workers, credit services companies, BBB, the World Wide Web, Chamber of Commerce, and your local library.*

America is the most diversified and exciting job marketplace in the entire world, offering countless job titles. Times do change. The truth is, no matter what the statistics state or a company's present position, employers will always keep one eye open for that special person who might make the difference for them. Interestingly, most people spend more time planning a vacation then they do in planning their career. Consider the importance on how a successful plan will determine your lifestyle and every financial decision that is ever made for you and your family. Its been said that there are three different types of people in this world: those who make things happen; those who watch things happen;

and those who ask "what happened?". We trust that you will gain a healthy edge over most job seekers after completing this book and begin taking advantage of the exercises references and resources that I make available.

With having a poor economy, deregulation, mergers, downsizing, and mass layoffs -- more and more people are out of work, all-the-while fewer and fewer jobs are being created and made available. Although as we continually move through the age of technology, most jobs will be in the service industry or in replacement jobs. Studies have shown that those who have neither the money nor the opportunity to get a degree, and many pay as much or more than jobs that require them. The US Department of Labor's Bureau of Labor Statistics report the difference is insignificant at best. Moreover, acquiring a college degree for high level roles is not enough. Many companies are now requesting additional degrees (with an emphasis on high GPA scores), as well as a minimum requirement of recent exposure to the field your applying. One job counselor commented that most large companies will not make the time to interview candidates with low GPAs, and will sometimes ask for a transcript. There is a multi-million-dollar entertainment company that has a specially designed fax machine that has specific keywords programmed in it, as well as a spell/grammar-check that automatically rejects resumes that don't meet up to their standards. Several issues may tend to make the job search a bit more challenging, but don't take rejections personally. J. W. Marriott once said, "Good timber does not always grow with ease; the greater the wind, the greater the tree's." Just as in his quote, the strong trees stood up to the strong winds, so must you stand up when being excluded. <u>Vow to Endeavor to Persevere</u>!

The question that may be racing through your mind is "Where do I start"? Perhaps the best place to start the search is with yourself. Are you willing to prepare for the role and do whatever it takes to help yourself, regardless of the sacrifices? Have you ever said to yourself "I'd rather be doing? (you fill in the blank); or… "I wonder if there's a person/place out there that will pay me for doing this"? Why not pursue a role that brings you pleasure now while you have the chance verses letting more time (years) in your life go by unsatisfied? What is it deep in your heart/mind that you always wanted to do or be? What stirs your blood the most when you think about it? Do you have a natural talent, skill or hobby that is or can be turned into a paid occupation? One career management consultant stated when sharing what companies are looking for in potential employees' is', *"After, knowledge, skills and attitude, companies look for dependability, dedication, new ways at looking at problems, strong in interpersonal skills, and the ability to work on a team."*

Be aware that Employers or prospects are not guidance counselors, and normally place you where you are needed rather than where you desire to be. If you're in school or presently employed, take advantage of the services provided, otherwise there are several local, state and government agencies that will help you. Begin in a library or on the internet, but do your homework and get started somewhere. Several suggestions are listed in the "Reference" chapter in the back of this book for your convenience. But beware, Consultants state there are risks involved for those who are presently employed and searching. Studies indicate that once you start to put the word out on the street that you looking elsewhere, it is only a matter of time before the word gets back to your employer. They state it takes approximately 12 weeks when calling or mailing resumes, only 4-6 weeks when you actually start meeting prospects (times may vary depending on the type and location of occupation), and the quickest.

Once you've selected the role(s) which (your experience should reflect a diversity of different job titles) you want to pursue, you must show how you're qualified to do it. Recall all former jobs and roles, training, schooling, military service, summer work, even family projects that can contribute towards your goal. Reflect upon your background to reveal everything noteworthy that will indicate to prospective employers that your more than capable of doing the intended role. The idea here is to prove that you can step right onto the role and perform effectively, or that your easily trainable and won't need extra supervision.

**Service Industry,** most people in the work force are in one way or another are or will be there whether it's restaurant or hotel or the travel industry etc. Your potential Employer is looking for people whom are friendly and reliable and customer service orientated and have the patience and tolerance to deal with the Public. For example, we "all" have come across that one person whom is hard to please and would rather make others feel bad – a Candidate needs to prove by the tone and cadence and pitch and choice of words to convince them you are seasoned and know how to defuse a negative situation and make it a positive one.

**Salesman** know that their main objective is not in selling the product, rather in selling themselves to the clients. Likewise, so it is with the job search and interview. Remember, it's critically important that you portray the attitude you're not simply looking to get something from the employer, *Rather,* you must persuade them that you are honestly interested in serving their customers with their best interest at heart, and do it sincerely! Try to live out that eternally inspiring phrase by J.F.K. "ask not what your country (company) can do for you, ask what can I do for my country (company)". Most importantly, you need to prove you will increase their bottom line – *money*, which you can do by building multiple professional relationships'. They have to feel it (that you care').

So, what do you do now with all the information you've collected? You market yourself, to which the avenues in the job search goes deep and wide. One successful option is in **"Networking"** (cold calling and not to be confused with Network Cards -- a index card with a short synopsis of oneself and one's abilities) which may be your best bet initially since approximately 75% of jobs are secured without any advertising whatsoever by the employer. It can be considered a numbers game, whereby the more people you contact and make aware of your situation -- the more opportunities will be made available and increase the possibility of securing a job. You can start with family and friends; then seek out co-workers, neighbors, job placement services, the daily newspapers, business associates, your rolodex and telephone book, periodicals and journals, the yellow pages, the internet, e-mail, people at school and church, political officers, job fairs, local unemployment office, or in casual conversations anywhere. Jack Lemmon once said, "if you have trouble meeting people, pick up someone else's golf ball". You may even want to consider a Temp Agency. The National Association Of Temporary Services' claims that approximately 29% of people who took a job through a temp agency were eventually hired in to full-time employment with the company that hired them on a permanent basis – and that's not bad.

For some, the job search can be an overwhelmingly lonely endeavor. One option could be is to recruit some help -- a "Coach" if you will, to guide, encourage, and council you. Pick someone close who is committed to your success and has the time to assist and hold you accountable and work with you until you find a successful position.

A survey conducted by the AARP of executives over 50 years old, had rated them high on their skills, work experience, and business ethics. However, they were unfortunately given a low rating on flexibility and adaptability when it came to technology related to computers. Ones heart goes out to these people who after serving faithfully whom having so much to offer, and are asked to step aside because their employers are feeling threatened for their own jobs. However, because of the ever-growing job place apathy epidemic, the latest statistics show that many companies having regret letting some of these great people go, are offering them their jobs back and some are offering re-signing bonus', and/or a raise to lure them back.

**Military** personnel who are now seeking civilian employment may feel a bit ill-equipped to make the transition and find it difficult to land a decent job. I have provided resources to aid those in these predicaments in the Reference section of TOMI. However, most Branches of the Service do offer a Job Placement Department – be sure to use it.

**Retired Athletes**, yes – most prefer and or need a job to have an income after their professional career is over, I recommend a Sports Agent' similar to the made famous' Dicky Fox in the popular Movie, Jerry McGuire. There a few Companies listed in the Resource's segment of this book for a starting point.

**Computer Guru's** out there, the training is so vast now, you'd be pressed as to where you want to start. However, there now are over 30 Colleges that offer computer subjects known as "Cyber skills" (on-line) classes, and the number is growing rapidly. The American Council on Education is said to be currently setting up guidelines for certification and degree's, which will certainly look impressive on any resume. These skills are not mandatory everywhere as yet, but it seems clear that they will be in vogue in the near future.

**Bankers** need to know and hear what a study done by The Economist Intelligence Unit of Coopers & Lybrand Consulting reported. Commenting on retail banking, they stated that "Staff reductions of as high as 50% by 2005 will not be uncommon." The study was based on interviews with over 50 banks internationally which predicts a change in response to changing customer needs, and replace staff with electronic devices.
On the other hand, maybe it's important to think small. According to MDR Demographic Applications and the Census

Bureau, jobs with companies who employ less than 100 people showed an increase of 28.1% or an 11.4 million people.

**Home based** businesses seem to be taking off by storm lately, and much can be said for the rewards both financially as well as personally. Are you a self-starter and like working unconventional hours? Do you enjoy working alone, really? Would everyday chores, phone calls, children, etc., interfere with your work? Do you honestly want to work alone. Do you have the office equipment needed and a means to all important information at home? Do you have a positive attitude, organizational skills, and the ability to schedule accordingly? If you answered yes to these questions, this just may be the thing for you.

Keep in mind that regardless of where your presently well in your career or just getting started - neither give up nor feel you'll never get ahead. John Dunlap -- the Tire king, was a veterinarian; King Gillette -- the Razor magnet, was a Cork salesman; and George Eastman -- the Kodak camera kingpin, was a bookkeeper!

# THE ONE MINUTE INTERVIEW
## CHAPTER III

### THE RESUME - *PLUS*

In this Chapter, I'll cover the do's and don'ts of your Resume preparation -- the Plus refers to those additional areas that when used in its entirety will give you edge over the competition.

What do you feel needs to be on a resume, and what should you include/exclude? What have you done, and what would look good? Perhaps the best way to answer these questions is, "What do employers really look for in a resume?" Since experts claim that all an applicant gets is a 10-20 second scan per resume, it's imperative you create it an appealing way. It must sizzle with excitement, and jump out right at them through the collage of clutter – since you only get one shot. Present yourself in such a way that you appear interesting enough to cause the reader to want to meet you. The art of the job is to collect all the data, then organize in a way so that it both amplifies your abilities as well as looks attractive to prospects in a way that will stand head and shoulders above the rest. Your goal here is to invite an interview, and by getting your foot in the door – your half the way there. There's far too much information already available at the bookstores by professionals, but there is a few basics I would like to cover (I have provided additional resources in the resource section in TOMI for your assistance).

## *The Resume*

Don't be normal and don't be boring - the old adage is true, Stand Out among the Rest! The best advice I could share would be to give your resume a KISS (keep it short and simple). If its too long, or disjointed, chances are it will not be read (would you?), and filed in the trash. Unless you're a specialist or top executive where your trade demands a detailed portfolio, try to keep it all one page. Have access to a computer with a high-quality printer (laser jet), or have a professional do it (normally costs about $50.00). Match the style of the resume that combines your personality with the position your pursuing. For example, if your interested in marketing -- use colored paper and include some graphics; if you're into journalism -- use poetic language and perhaps offer a sample; etc. Use your imagination and be original – be you! Walk their walk and talk their talk.

In general, a inviting resume should include the following: prepared on normal white/off white 8.5" x 11" 24 lb. premium paper with matching envelopes if mailing (be sure to type the envelope); Again, be different to get their attention, such as colored paper or colored ink verses all black ink, if it is appropriate and you have the confidence include a facial picture; have a balance and a natural flow with some blank space so as not to appear cluttered; use a asterisk to highlight (bullet) specific achievements (projects, creations, increased sales/decreased costs, etc.), headings to qualifications and experience, degrees, languages, certification, or honors; use positive, easy to read short sentences -- keep in mind a resume is not an autobiography, rather a sales brochure -- and your the product. Highlight strengths and downplay or reword weaknesses to your advantage; to those who served time -- state any experience or education received, or any certification to your advantage. Include a "pinch of linguistic intrepidity with a dash of ledger domain". What I mean is, use keywords and phrases that sound impressive, and by no means make any typos or grammatical errors. Do not include: salary requirements or history (unless directly asked to); multiple employers or explanations for leaving companies; any non-business related information or dishonest statements; or personal references (reserve these until the after the interview). It's also ok to have more than one different types of resumes, and try to keep it updated recurrently.

The immediate goal is to get a copy of your resume in the hands of the person to who makes the hiring decisions. Please review some of the examples included. You may even want to do a video resume if you can afford - it and look good on TV and perform well. For additional help, start with some friends, go to the local library, or seek professional services if you can afford it.

If you feel confident and the job you're applying for would welcome it, it might help your chances to put your photo in the upper corner at the front page of Resume. It will help do just what you want your Resume to do – stand out enough get the hiring managers attention.

### *Cover Letter*

Alongside the resume, you may choose to include a cover letter that amplifies your qualifications to aid your goal of getting an interview. Keep in mind that managers are not only busy people and have much more responsibilities than hiring, but also will most likely have a stack full applicants to go through. Therefore, your first sentence needs to be eye-catching in order to grab their full attention, telling them actually what you want to say -- to the point, better still – what they want to hear! The second paragraph should state the position your applying for, and how you found out about the position. You may include the name(s) of references you have that are currently employed there, but be sure they are in good standing. Next, get to the heart of the matter, state your qualifications in a more practical way then stated on your resume. Include accomplishment and responsibilities, clubs and organizations you belong to, and any additional skills that would enhance your qualifications to make you stand out head and shoulders above the crowd. Close the letter with a final salutation, to include a request to have them call to schedule an interview. Refer to the sample we included for an example to get yours started.

## *Self-Marketing Options*

As an additional option, "Network Cards" are sometimes used to advertise oneself to potential employers. How it works is, you take a 3"x 5" index card, list your name -- address -- telephone #, the type of position desired, and a brief description of your qualifications. The object is to circulate these to everyone you know, and place them everywhere you can. Some people take this one step further using a "Self-Marketing Letter" to send to contacts and friends as well as ads. Typed on normal size paper, this format usually starts off with personal salutation or form of reference. This informs its reader that you are seeking work (specify what area), and to keep their eyes open for you should they hear of something within your field. For those who chose to supplement their search with these options, I would suggest that you stay in constant contact with those to whom you mailed.

## *References*

Most companies will ask for list of references so they can contact them to verify you in a variety of ways. You can submit friends you know that will give a positive profile of you, but it would be to your advantage if you could include influential contacts within the community or present employees that work at the intended company. Almost every application will have a section for these however it will look more professional if you have them pre-typed on a separate piece of paper. Bring this with you on the interview, but don't offer it unless asked. Moreover, it is suggested that you do not fill in their names on anything, rather to write in "on file" or "upon request". Remember, you need to protect these contacts, and submit them only to companies you feel are serious about hiring you. Your references are busy people too and don't need to be bothered by every place you apply, just the serious ones. Besides, you want to keep a healthy relationship with your contacts. You do not want them to feel over burdened in helping you, rather to appear fresh and excited by the caller. But make sure you first get their approval, as well as provide them what they might expect to say. Don't forget, if any of them were a decidable influence in landing a job, you owe them one.

### *Letter of Reference*

What I refer to here is an accumulated list of letters addressed to you by clients and customers, who give a positive reflection on your services to them and/or their company. Keep only the ones not only specifically designate you, but also include performance, leadership, and accomplishments that created a win-win situation. Collect these to save for your portfolio and during your interviews submit them at the appropriate time, you'll find this may just be the edge you'll need to land the job.

### *Thank-You Letter*

I guarantee that if you do this, you will stand out about 50% above the competition because many people – over 50% neglect to do this simple exercise. Some Managers use this as a test to see not only if you're genuinely interested in coming to work for them, but also they use this as an example of your skill set and business ethics. It's really true that sometimes "actions speak louder than words"! Therefore, after meeting or talking to the interviewer (prospective employer), it is both courteous and advantageous to send a thank-you letter in addition to even follow-up with a phone call if you feel good about it.

Your opening statement should be personal, indicating the shared experience in order to establish a growing professional relationship. A short and simple sentence like "I would like to thank you for making the time to meet with me on Monday, as it was a pleasure to meet you". Your letter should be direct, positive, enthusiastic, and definitely express that the role is more than interesting to you. It will be acceptable to restate your background and accomplishments, but don't be redundant. Word them in a way that will reflect your compatibility in a positive fashion with the role and company. Close with your personal salutations and ask for a return call, or state that you'll be making one for an update on hiring status (add your own personality and be sure to customize the letter per your interaction). It is to your advantage to prepare the letter as soon as possible after the interview is over - while it's still fresh on your mind (and theirs). Mail it out the same day or the next morning at the very latest.

If you decide to make a call, make it from a quite location so as not to be disturbed. Write down in advance precisely what to say, practice it over and over until you feel comfortable enough for the actual call. You may want to include asking if they had made a decision, and if not - if you're still a candidate or if a second interview would be in order. Keep in mind that although your call is appreciated, it is an unexpected interruption, so speak clearly, calmly and to the point. You don't want to be an annoyance, rather one who is thorough, decisive, and sincere.

## *Acceptance Letter*

In an effort to show the consistency of your professionalism, this letter will welcome you officially to the company. It's also a written form to document the verbal offer and agreement. Wait until you are actually offered the job first, keep it brief -- to a few short sentences, then mail it the same day, no later! Again, keep it simple, begin by thanking them for their time, the pleasure in meeting them, and for the offer. Your next sentence should cut to the matter "At this time I wish to formally announce that I will accept the (fill in the position) offered, effective (fill in the date)". If your confidence is high, you can add some suggestions on how you will contribute to the goals of the company, and what you can bring to the table. Close with a general statement like "Look forward to working together", or "I look forward to a long working relationship", use your own personality.

### *Letter of Resignation*

It might prove to your advantage to keep on file copies of submitted resumes in case a future employer requests additional information of separation. Unlike the other letters we covered, this can be as long as you wish in order to convey your feelings and reasons for separation. It will look favorably if you can give the standard two-week notice, specifying the final date and time of your last day there. There are formulas out there that will advise on how it should be written, but I would suggest you keep it short, professional, and non-discriminatory. In the event you were let go (for any reason) try not to mention names or specifics, and word things in a way that indicate you were not to blame, rather a victim. Be sure not to bash anyone nor the company. Instead, reflect on ways that how your former company led/paved the way for what you really wanted (the new job you secured or are searching for).


## 5 Quick Points about Your Resume

1. <u>Objective</u>.
First impressions are very important as this may be the single chance you will get to capture the attention of the

interviewer. Do your best to sell yourself by including top highlights and achievements, training and education, and various elements of your prior experience that will relate to the position you're applying for. Keep it to a short paragraph, and be sure to customize each section for different job titles.

2. <u>Experience</u>.
Start off by listing your previous position starting from your current or last one. Include your title, name of the company, dates of employ, and a solid paragraph your job description. Most importantly be honest, remember it can be verified.

3. <u>Education, Certification, Membership</u>
Too much education may date' you or even appear overqualified, and if you have none don't lie rather amplify on your experience and qualifications. Be balanced and remember this may get verified. Be sure to include all Certifications achieved as even if they don't fit the position it may be important to the interviewer. Former and current Memberships will show involvement and impact into the community, and just may the deciding factor.

4. <u>Content</u>
Be concise and use power words that fit the role, and be sure include Key Words that were in their ad for that role. I don't recommend putting down salary requirements or history, nor personal references. Let them ask, it will help foster a longer conversation later. Be sure to put the best way to contact you and include an email address, it has been suggested to put these along with your name in a different color soas it will stand out.

5. <u>Design</u>
Interviewers will make a quick judgment about you immediately by the layout of your resume, as they don't have the time to read everything. Avoid overdoing it with fancy paper or print, and remember the KISS maxim. Stick to the facts, and add in a % or $ symbols where you can – they draw attention and curiosity. Save the details for the interview.

# THE ONE MINUTE INTERVIEW CHAPTER THREE REVIEW

"The Resume - Plus"

**The Resume**

**Cover letter**

**Self-Marketing Options**

**References**

**Letter of Reference**

**Thank You Letter**

**Acceptance Letter**

**Letter of Resignation**

# THE ONE MINUTE INTERVIEW
## CHAPTER IV

**THE INTERVIEW**

*This chapter is not only the heart of this book, but also the most important fascist of the entire Job Search' process. The main thing you need to keep in mind as to why you were called in for an interview is... they are bringing you in to determine if you will "fit" in with the team or program/organization. This may mean one's gender, nationality, personality/character traits, or sometimes to see if your smarter than they are. I've personally lost several opportunities (as did many of you) because the interviewer was intimidated by me and didn't hire me in fear of losing their job. Believe this happens more often than you may initially think. Remember, your already qualified for the position, or else they would not of called you in and wasted both of your time. Henry Ford said, "whether you think you can or you can't – your right". Let's face Everyone makes mistakes, everyone wants to be the ideal candidate, your job is to learn from them and make less than the others. Not just act confident Be Confident! Have the Confidence that you will acquire a job somewhere eventually and maybe, just maybe the organization you were hoping to join would not have turned out the best for you in a variety of ways.*

### *Common Ground*

Do this and you may be hired on the spot! I once was in conversation with a Vice President of a company, and during the interview it came up that we some of the same people in the business as well as positions we held and locations we formally worked at. At the end of the interview (rather he purposely cut it short) he hired me on the spot. So to begin with, not only listen intently to reflect upon/if there are similarities worth mentioning, but also if things around the office or in the area, anything to create fun–common small talk. This will give you an edge, and create a calm feeling in the air. That you have similarities, things in common, part of the team – you're half way there. For example, if you live/lived in the area – comment on some highlights of the area, even if you've never been there before – comment on how nice the area is. If you see a plaque on the wall that is familiar to one you have, or something in their office or on their desk. Like, a sports picture, ocean, whatever it is find something in common with you and talk about! But do this either before or after the actual sit-down interview – never-ever during unless they bring it up.

**Smile-Smile-Smile**

The first and foremost important factor to do is smile! If you get nothing else from this entire book, please remember to smile at the beginning when you meet, smile during and throughout the interview, and smile when your shaking hands goodbye. This single action may make or break it. Moreover, bring a fresh copy (several) of your resume, and other documents that will aid you in selling yourself. To begin with, have a great opening statement like, "thank you for inviting me to come in today. I've been looking forward to meeting you/this interview since our last conversation (or simply say the day you spoke). Don't' answer questions to quickly, a momentary pause increases stature, not to mention gives you additional time to think. Also, don't tell or make jokes, nor offer too much small talk during silent moments. If you're being interview by several different people before being hire – be sure to provide the same information and documentation, although find an independent common ground with them as well. If it's a phone interview, have all the necessary information laid out before you so your ready for anything and not appearing to scramble carelessly. In general, be in control of yourself, but leave control and the direction of the interview solely in the hands of the interviewer.

## *Interviewing is a Craft*

Tony Curtis used to say, "when I go to work in a movie, all I want to be is just a little bit better than what is expected of me. That's the way I've tried to live my life too". Job interviewing has by some – been compared to as performance acting and/or drama. The idea here is not to be phony, vein or dishonest, rather to be as natural as possible in a new setting. No one is perfect, we all know that, but keep in mind you only have approximately thirty minutes to communicate your entire business life to a total stranger. One way to overcome is to practice. Start in front of a mirror, or preferably ask some of you're your friends to role-play – you'll uncover blind spots in your presentation. "Practice make Permanent"!

## *Dress for Success*

Do First Impressions Matter? You had better believe they do! We've all heard the phrase "clothes make the man", the same goes for the job place – dress for the part. If it's business office, wear a suit and bring a briefcase, if a shop – blue jeans. If you are unsure, go there a couple days before and scope things out. The general rule still applies, when in doubt – overdress a notch. Think ahead, most people wouldn't go out on a date dressed inappropriately, otherwise your date may decide to go out with someone who can dress nice - you get the picture. Your appearance makes a subtle statement, and makes the kind of initial positive impression you need to have. Look fresh, lively, act as though you enjoy yourself, a fun and interesting person to be around - sell yourself to yourself first and foremost.

## *Body Language*

The first moments you meet, and the first few minutes you talk are the most important of the entire interview. Studies show that communication is 20% verbal & 80% non-verbal - the eyes especially cannot lie. For many years' law enforcement agencies have utilized Physiology studies prove that when under questioning, if one's eyes go up and to the left, your accessing the visual cortex and therefore telling the truth because your remembering an actual event. However, if your eyes go up and to the right, your accessing the creative side of the brain – (an event that didn't happen) and therefore telling a lie. Moreover, if you cough, sneeze, cross your legs, scratch your face, a small smirk, uneasy look, look away, and even a blink in your eyes will give you away. With this in mind, believe that how you (and your body) communicate is more important that what you say. Again, they already have all the facts about you from the resume and reference checks – this is the final hurdle. Sometimes it may pay off to show your similarity with the interviewer by mirror them. Imitate their gestures, laugh, mannerisms, etc, this will subconsciously show you are the same and can therefore get along well. Broadway man Damon Runyon said, "the job offer goes not always to those we like, nor the hiring of our twins, but that's the way to bet".

Writer – actor and director Ken Delmar teaches in his series "Winning Moves", states for you to send in a character to go in and act for you! Use a key – picture image – word that is fast and quick that will remind you of that character instantly. This character must be a renown respected and successful person and if possible someone you know personally.

### Questions and Answers

Good questions will show interest in the position and firm, and knowledge of the position you're applying for. Conversely, bad questions like asking for a immediate decision, days and hours, benefits and salary - you need to stay clear of unless initiated by them and your simply asking for clarity only. Have ready in your mind to answer any question they can throw out at you. For example, if you are applying for a managerial position whereby you will be managing people, you can expect the question, "what is your management style"? You should be prepared for an answer such as meets the job profile. For most office situations you can try, "I lead boldly yet speak softly. I treat my staff with respect, while expecting excellence and empowering them to deliver". Back in College, I sometimes studied for exams by writing out potential questions that could be covered. At first it was hit and miss, but by the forth year I sometimes had every question covered in some form or another. Therefore, be ready to answer the basics such as: describe your average day; three strengths and weaknesses; why your looking for a new/different job; how you have/will respond to different situations; provide information about prior positions/companies you worked for; etc. Remember, never bring up or ask about salary/bonus's sick -pay, or benefits. Be careful here because you will be judged by the questions you ask - so think it through before your interview. Also, some companies do additional things such as a background search, credit check, personality and competency testing, as well as drug tests. Aristotle said, "excellence isn't a single act, it is what you repeatedly do". James D. Kohlmann – a Miami executive recruiter said, "in the thousands of interviews I have evaluated with hiring managers, never once have I heard one of them say, "I don't want that fellow, he's too interested in the work". For additional help, I have provided several samples in Chapter Five "Exercises and Study Guides".

## *Put yourself in their shoes*

We all know that being put on the spot – will cause us to fear, however there are many things you can do to overcome this. But don't think for one minute the interviewer isn't just as uncomfortable as you are. Just because you don't have a job or are the one doing the hunting, you alone will be nervous. No-No-No. As seasoned as I am - as are others, I still feel alittle uncomfortable sometimes. So, don't come across that you need this job secured today or your committing suicide. Rather, portray enough confidence in yourself to leave them with the impression they would be crazy not to hire you ASAP. Moreover, the interviewer typically has many other functions that they need to be performing and most of the time would prefer the process to go as swiftly and painlessly as possible. Remember they have people they have to report to as well, and not only need to be thorough, but also timely.

### Exit Well

Be sure to be bold enough to call him/her to a commitment i.e., "when will you be making your decision", or "when can I expect to hear from you", "by what date do you intend to fill this by/on", or (again add you own personality). You need to get this important fact for two reasons: so you know how to plan out your ongoing search, and it shows sincere interest in the position. Keep your smile - poise and composure all the way out the door and to your car. As the interview is escorting you out, sometimes it pays off to make polite comments on the property or amplifying on something you talked about, and sometimes it's better off not to say anything - you decide. Don't except an offer on the spot, unless you absolutely sure this is for you and your comfortable with things. It can be an honest issue, but chances are it will show desperation on either or both parts, and maybe there's more than meets the eye in a negative fashion – beware and wise, but make your decision in a timely fashion. Show some penuche - don't (appear) be overly anxious, let them pursue you a bit and make them really want you (you got it – just like dating).

### After The Interview

After the interview is over, be sure to recap the meeting on paper, to cover your personal strengths and weaknesses and better yourself next time out. Also, be sure to send off a thank you letter or call the next day – the latest. It's acceptable to call once a week or so and ask for an update on a job that is not opening up immediately, but don't be a burden by overdoing it – you can tell by the reception and tone of voice when you call. If you get a call within a week or so, or within the time they mentioned when you ask them – even if it's just for more information or an update – your chances are increasing on getting the job. On the other hand, if days go by and there's no contact - rather a letter in the mail – yep – it's a dear John. Keep in mind that even though you can be well prepared, have all the answers, dress well, come across very polished, but still not land the job. But try not to beat yourself up, the reasons can be as deep and wide as an ocean. Keep a positive outlook, and remember that victory will come to the one who gets up one more time than being knocked down.

### *After Landing the Job*

There once was a man who upon starting at his new job, was met by the person he was replacing. The outgoing employee said it has been an ongoing tradition that three envelopes numbered one – two –and three get passed along to the new people. What you do he said, is whenever you get into trouble open up an envelope respectively at each incident. So, everything started off ok, but after a short time he made a mistake and got in trouble, so he opened up the first envelope - It read, "blame it on the former manager", so he did, which that worked for a while and everything was fine. Then, as you would have it, a little bit down the road he made another mistake which got him in trouble again - so he opened the second envelope - It read, "blame it on your staff", so that's just what he did. Well that worked for a while and everything was fine but as his luck would have it, a little further down the road he made another mistake and got him in trouble again, so, he opened the third and final envelope and it read, "make out three envelopes". The moral of the story is…. (you fill in the blank!).

# THE ONE MINUTE INTERVIEW
# CHAPTER FOUR REVIEW

"The Interview"

**Common ground**

**Smile-Smile-Smile**

**Interviewing is a craft**

**Dress for success**

**Body language**

**Questions and Answers**

**Put yourself in their shoes**

**Exit well**

**After the interview**

**After landing the job**

# ONE MINUTE INTERVIEW
## CHAPTER V

## EXERCISES

The following will be a variety of exercises - informative lists - statistics, quotes, and a variety of information for your easy reference - study and preparation. They will enhance your ability to communicate more efficiently during your interview. Keep in mind a few simple principles before you answer:

- Be Clear - on what the question is, it's easy to be misunderstood
- Be Certain - of yourself, answer calmly, smoothly, and clearly
- Be Confident - you do know your job and your abilities
- Be Confidential - don't be negative, opinionated, or derogatory
- Be Complimentary - everyone loves to hear a genuine compliment

**CHANCES ARE**

Most people who get this wrong:

Fill in the blanks.
1. My name is _____
2. I work for _____
3. My salary is paid by_____

Answers: 1. Your own name, 2. My customers, 3. My customers.

**This is a timed test - you only have three minutes.**
(Do you remember this tricky one!?)

1. Read everything carefully before you start.
2. Put your name in the upper right - hand corner.
3. Circle the word "name" in line two.
4. Draw four small squares in the upper left corner of the page.
5. Now put a check-mark in each square.
6. Sign your name on the back of the page.
7. Put a circle around the number seven.
8. Put a question mark in the lower left corner.
9. Now draw a star around the mark you just made.
10. Turn the page over and do the math to multiple 71 x 17.
11. Draw a rectangle around the word "star in line nine.
12. Turn the page over again and add 45,551 + 89,694.
13. Now circle your answer.
14. Underline all odd numbers on the page.
15. Now that you have finished reading everything carefully, do only lines one and two.

Do you remember getting caught at one like this? Now recall the embarrassment!? This old - simple and yet effective little quiz says it all for what I want to communicate in this chapter. PAY ATTENTION!!! IT will make you (your career) - or break you (your career).

**Your attitude is also very important. Complete this next exercise as honestly as you can - see how you rate.**

Read the following questions below and circle the number you feel is where you currently are. Five being the highest and one being the lowest.

1. My boss would rate my current attitude as       5
          4        3       2       1
2. My friends and family would rate me a          5
          4        3       2       1

3. I would honestly rate my current attitude as a    5
          4        3        2        1
4. My attitude towards people in general is    5
          4        3        2        1
5. My motivation and creativity level is    5
          4        3        2        1
6. My general sense of humor is    5
          4        3        2        1
7. My level of patience and sensitivity to others is    5
          4        3        2        1
8. I let things bother me    5
          4        3        2        1
9. I receive complaints from others    5
          4        3        2        1
10. My enthusiasm for my job and me life is    5
          4        3        2        1
11. I able to control my own mood    5
          4        3        2        1
12. I'm pleasant to people who are not to me    5
          4        3        2        1
13. I enjoy meeting new people    5
          4        3        2        1
14. I admit when I'm wrong    5
          4        3        2        1
15. I'm always trying to improve my people skills    5
          4        3        2        1
16. I enjoy serving others who need the help    5
          4        3        2        1
17. I'm good at remembering people's names    5
          4        3        2        1
18. Other peoples time is important to me    5
          4        3        2        1
19. Try to see the good side of people    5
          4        3        2        1
20. I keep myself in good shape and clean hygiene    5
          4        3        2        1

If you scored a b/w 90-100: you have great customer service and people skills - and have a highly positive outlook on life

- keep it up! If you scored b/w 70 - 89 you're middle of the road - easy going. However, you may need to watch yourself at times, remember your boss is always evaluating you. If you scored b/w 41 - 69 you have a lot of work to do in order to be successful in the marketplace, consider seeking professional advice. If you scored below 40, quit your job and stay in bed - you're only headed for trouble!

## On a scale of one to five circle the level you feel your closet to (five being the highest)

Rate your varied abilities on how well you know yourself.

1. When communicating with others I generally make a good first impression, put them at ease.
   *1     2     3     4     5*

2. It's natural for me to want to help people and make them feel comfortable in talking with me.
   *1     2     3     4     5*

3. I am at-ease with influencing people and moving them from their point of view to another.
   *1     2     3     4     5*

4. I am more than qualified to lead and motivate people cooperatively toward a common goal.
   *1     2     3     4     5*

5. I have strong clerical abilities and a systematic method of organizing - scheduling and filing.
   *1     2     3     4     5*

6. I have a general understanding of basic mechanics - and/or can easily figure things out.
   *1     2     3     4     5*

8. I have good hand-to-eye coordination and manual dexterity.
   *1    2    3    4    5*

9. Numbers - formulas - figures and problem solving are routine for me.
   *1    2    3    4    5*

10. I am creative and enjoy drawing - painting - arts and music.
    *1    2    3    4    5*

11. I prefer to express myself through writing and literary arts.
    *1    2    3    4    5*

## Here's another personality questionnaire. Be sure to keep track of your answers to tabulate your score.

1. When do you feel your best?
a. in the morning    b. during the day    c. late at night

Do you usually walk?
a. quickly with long steps b. quickly with short steps c. casually head up d. casually head down e. slowly

3. When you talk with people, do you typically?
fold your arms b. clamp your hands c. hands in pockets or on hips d. touchy e. itchy

4. When sitting, do you?
a. bend your knees to your side b. cross your legs c. legs are stretched d. one leg bent

5. If you find something funny, do you?
a. laugh loudly  b. average laugh  c. more of a chuckle d. simply grin

6. When going to a party, you usually?

a. make a noticeable entrance b. look for someone familiar c. quiet and don't really mingle well

7. If you're in the middle of a work project and are interrupted, do you?
a. welcome the interruption b. get really upset c. are evenly balanced

8. Which of the following colors do you like?
a. red/orange b. black c. yellow/light blue d. green e. dark blue/purple f. white g. brown/gray

9. When you go to sleep, do you?
a. stretched out face up b. stretched out face down c. on your side/curled d. face to arm e. under the covers

10. When you dream, you usually are?
a. falling b. brawling or struggling c. seem to be searching d. flying e. dreamless f. peaceful/calm

Add up your points as follows:
**1**. (a) 2; (b) 4; (c) 6     **2**. (a) 6; (b) 4; (c) 7; (d) 2; (e) 1 **3**. (a) 4; (b) 2; (c) 5; (d) 7; (e) 6
**4**. (a) 4; 5. (b) 6; (c) 2; (d) 1     **5**. (a) 6; (b) 4; (c) 3; (d) 5; (e) 2     **6**. (a) 6; (b) 4; (c) 2
**7**. (a) 6; (b) 2; (c) 4     **8**. (a) 6; (b) 7; (c) 5; (d) 4; (e) 3; (f) 2; (g) 1
**9**. (a) 7; (b) 6; (c) 4; (d) 2; (e) 1 **10**. (a) 4; (b) 2; (c) 3; (d) 5; (e) 6; (f) 1

Over 60 Points:
Some people may believe you to be a one who is self-centered and dominating, while others may admire your strength and desire to be more like you. In either case, you may appear one to be on your toes around. Some may not choose to get too close to you, as they won't trust you fully.

Between 51-60 Points
You may be perceived to be a person with natural leadership abilities - one quick to make a decision. Possessing an exciting, yet sometimes impulsive personality - a bit bold and

one who likes to take chances and therefore enjoy being in your company.

Between 41-50 Points
People see you as a charming person - upbeat, interesting, considerate of others, and in general quite fun to be around. You are well liked by most people and easily make and keep friends.

Between 31-40 Points
Most people may see you as being well balanced - cautious, sensible, pragmatic, one who is gifted, witty, loyal, and modest. In your inner circle of family and friends - you both trust them and are well trusted. However, if/when disappointed by them it takes longer to win back your trust.

Between 21-30 Points
People see you as detailed and thorough, as well as examining things carefully prior to making decisions. Also, you may be perceived as a bit anal, yet easy to get along with.

If you scored under 21 Points
You are perceived as being on the shy side and a little uneasy around people. Also, some people may see as being indecisive, quiet, a loner, perhaps a bit boring, and lacking in confidence.

**The following is a collection of various informative quick tips, phrases, and business principles. These can be an effective learning tool to improve your work ethic, increase your vocabulary, and enhance your level of professionalism. Remember, the choices we make day by day shape our lives - choose how you want to live now. Like the immortal saying goes: there are three kinds of people in the world; those who make things happen, those who watch things happen, and those who say "what happened". Which one are you?**

**Food - for - thought prior to the interview.**

1. My employer clearly defines goals and expectations of my level of performance.
2. I have been thoroughly and properly trained for the position I was hired for.
3. My input received and welcomed when I want to implement changes.
4. When being disciplined, I am usually approached in a healthy and supportive nature.
5. Conversely, I am recognized when goals are met, and positive achievements are made.
6. When I communicate with either my employer or employees, I am listened to intently.
7. I show and give mutual respect and recognition.

**Possible Interview Questions**

- What are your salary requirements?
- Are you willing to relocate?
- What are some of your motivations?
- What are some of your short/long term goals?
- Do you work well under pressure?
- What are some of your strengths and weaknesses?
- Are you creative, analytical, administrative, partisan, and/or a leader?
- How was the working relationship with your former/current employer?
- Why do you want to come to work for us?
- In what ways can you contribute to the company?
- How do you think you will fit in with our team?
- Why are you changing fields?
- To what level of experience do you have?
- Can we contact your former employer?
- What do your do in your spare time?
- What do you like best/least about your job?
- Why do you feel your qualified for a promotion?

- Tell me about the most rewarding project/accomplishment you've done.
- How soon are you looking to start?
- Why does it appear you change jobs frequently?
- Have you ever been fired, if so -why?
- Do you prefer working on your own or with others?
- Are there any travel or time or day - of - week limitations?
- Tell me about a bad situation, and what you did to remedy it.
- Why did you leave you last job/why are you looking?
- Define for me what customer service means to you.
- What would some of your employees/co-workers say about you?
- What is it about this business that excites you?
- Why should I select you for this position over someone else?
- Define your management style.
- What efforts do you do to keep/maintain moral?
- What time of the day are you at you best?
- Do you plan to move in the next five years?
- What do you think your current employer will say when you put in your notice?
- Tell me about your education/training/certificates.
- What is/was your GPA?
- Do you plan to further your education?
- What are some of your personal motivations?
- What is your current salary?
- How do you feel about working overtime?
- Do you have any questions for me?
- Is this a new position, or am I replacing someone?
- Is there anyone else I'll need to interview with for this position?
- When will you anticipate making your final decision?
- Will there be training involved?
- What will be my initial goals?
- Is there an immediate issue that needs to be addressed?

- How soon do you intend on filling the position?
- Will the company allow me to further my education?
- If hired, who would I report to?
- Explain the management flow - chart.
- If selected, when can I expect to hear from you?
- Can you describe for me what a typical day for me might be like?
- Do you have any other positions here that I might be qualified for?
- Are there opportunities for advancement?
- Who are the people I would potentially be working with?
- If hired, how would my performance be evaluated?
- Who owns the company/or the co. public/any stockholders?
- Are current sales/revenue/business as high as last year?
- Can I have a brief tour?
- Is there any company information I can take with me to read up on?
- When can I start?

## 5 Quick Points about Your Resume

1. <u>Objective</u>.
   First impressions are very important as this may be the single chance you will get to capture the attention of the interviewer. Do your best to sell yourself by including top highlights and achievements, training and education, and various elements of your prior experience that will relate to the position you're applying for. Keep it to a short paragraph, and be sure to customize this section for each different job title.
2. <u>Experience</u>.
   Start right off by listing your previous position starting from your current or last one. Include your title, name of the company, dates of employ, and a

solid paragraph your job description. Most importantly be honest, remember it can be verified.

3. <u>Education, Certification, Membership</u>
   Too much education may date' you or even appear overqualified, and if you have none don't lie rather amplify on your experience and qualifications. Be balanced and remember this may get verified. Be sure to include all Certifications achieved as even if they don't fit the position it may be important to the interviewer. Former and current Memberships will show involvement and impact into the community, and just may the deciding factor.

4. <u>Content</u>
   Be concise and use power words that fit the role, and be sure include Key Words that were in their ad for that role. I don't recommend putting down salary requirements or history, nor personal references. Let them ask, it will help foster a longer conversation later. Be sure to put the best way to contact you and include an email address, it has been suggested to put these along with your name in a different color soas it will stand out.

5. <u>Design</u>
   Interviewers will make a quick judgment about you immediately by the layout of your resume, as they don't have the time to read everything. Avoid overdoing it with fancy paper or print, and remember the KISS maxim. Stick to the facts, and add in a % or $ symbols where you can – they draw attention and curiosity. Save the details for the interview.

## 10 Telephone Sales Techniques

1. Smile – it will come across in your delivery.
2. Be mentally prepared, as you will be challenged with interesting questions.

3. Use their name as often as you can as it builds report and comforts them.
4. Answer their question with a question – it will keep the conversation going.
5. Be sure you know the client and their needs.
6. When the question on the price be sure to build in value before you answer.
7. Have all your facts and resources readily available.
8. Get them saying yes often as it builds a positive progression towards the sale.
9. Paint a word picture so they can see it in their mind as this adds value.
10. Never let them see (hear) you sweat.

## 10 Tips to Improve Rapport

1. Use Humor when you can
2. Lead the conversation
3. Use questions to motivate interest
4. Answer questions with questions
5. Share personal stories
6. Use their name often
7. Be sensitive to Hot-Buttons
8. Show empathy to relate
9. Ask open-ended questions
10. Listen! Listen! Listen!

## 20 Quick Tips for Sales People

- Ask for the sale
- Believe in yourself
- Believe in your product/service
- Feel good about the company you work for
- Be fully prepared
- Be on-time or slightly early for appointments
- Have a professional appearance

- Establish a rapport early on the conversation
- Use humor where and when appropriate
- Be fully knowledgeable with your product/service
- Have a detailed answer for every question raised
- Focus on the benefits, not the features
- Be completely honest
- Make only the promises you can keep
- Don't speak negatively about your competition
- Use examples and/or testimonies where possible
- Be a good listener
- Be alert to their buying signals
- Have a good answer for any/all objections
- ASK FOR THE SALE!

**Top 20 Ways To Close a Sale Almost Every Time**

1. Be on time! *There is no excuse to be late and it could be a deal breaker*
2. Make a great and lasting first impression! *You only get one chance to good impression*
3. Pre-Qualify the customer! *Be sure that they can use what your selling*
4. Dress appropriately! *It may vary per sales call, and it makes them feel comfortable*
5. Prepare yourself in advance! *Practice – Practice - Practice*
6. Give 100% of your effort! *Otherwise it may show, and it may just the edge you need*
7. Know your product intimately! *It can help build your confidence in the presentation*
8. Believe in your product with conviction! *If you don't, you can't expect them to*
9. Determine immediately how you can help them! *Look for common ground*
10. Immediately establish rapport! *Be a quick study of their office and use it*
11. Use Humor often! *It can help relieve stress and periods of silence*

12. Tell the truth! *Never lie, it could back to haunt you*
13. Don't down the competition! *Agree with the customer, it may prevent a disagreement*
14. Use testimonials – *Offer referrals to dispel objections*
15. If you make a promise, keep it! *Remember, your word is your bond*
16. Address any question or concern quickly and completely! *This helps build confidence*
17. Get them saying "Yes", throughout the presentation! *It helps build mental repetitions*
18. Watch and listen for positive signals! *Both body language and verbal cues*
19. Have a excellent closing! *Say it all with one closing statement and firmly*
20. Ask for the Sale! *Look them in the eye, smile, and don't speak until they do*


## CHOOSE ME FOR THE POSTION BECAUSE

- I am professionally trained and certified in …
- I have enjoyed a successful track record
- I can help make you/this company successful
- I was raised and lived in this area all my life
- I have a degree in…
- I can show you how to save on overhead
- I have several business associates/leads/contracts I can bring in with me
- I used to work here
- I am very experienced in…
- I'm from the old school
- I've been in this field for years
- I love my job


## IMPROVE YOUR LISTENING SKILLS BY

- Being prepared in advance

- Think like a customer
- Limit your talking
- Listen to what they're not saying
- Be alert to their tone on voice
- Concentrate solely on the call
- Don't ever interrupt
- Take copious notes
- Ask questions for clarification
- Use reflective phases in response
- Never - ever argue a point or issue
- Practice - practice - practice!

## BODY LAUNGUAGE SPEAKS VOLUMES

| WHAT YOU DO | WHAT IT SAYS |
|---|---|
| Making direct eye contact *assertive* | *Friendly, sincere, self-confident,* |
| Avoiding eye contact *passive* | *Insecure, evasive, indifferent,* |
| Shaking your head *disagreeing* | *Disagreeing, shocked,* |
| Patting on the back *consoling* | *Encouraging, congratulatory,* |
| Scratching your head *confused* | *Bewildered, disbelieving,* |
| Smiling *peaceful* | *Content, understanding,* |
| Biting your lip | *Nervous, anxious, uncertain* |
| Folding your arms *disapproving* | *Angry, disagreeing,* |
| Tapping your feet | *Nervous, anxious, uncertain* |
| Raising your eyebrows *concerned* | *Surprised, disbelieving,* |
| Narrowing eyebrows *disapproving* | *Angry, disagreeing,* |
| Wringing hands | *Upset, nervous, anxious* |

| | |
|---|---|
| Leaning forward | *Interested, attentive, anxious* |
| Slouching in your seat | *Bored, tired, relaxed* |
| Sitting on edge of seat | *Nervous, anxious, uncertain* |
| Shifting in seat | *Restless, bored, anxious* |
| Hunched over | *Exhausted, insecure, passive* |
| Erect posture | *Refined, self-confident, assertive* |

## THE TONE OF VOICE

It's not so much what you say,
As is the manner in which you say it.
It's not so much the language you use,
As the tone in which you convey it.
"Come here", I sharply said,
And the child coward and wept,
"Come here", I said,
He looked and smiled,
and straight to my lap he crept.
Words may be mild and fair,
But the tone may piece like a dart.
Words may be as soft as the summer air,
But the tone may break my heart.
For words come from the mind,
Crafted by time and art.
But tone leaps from the inner self,
Revealing the true state of heart.
Whether you know it or not,
Whether you mean it or care,
Gentleness, kindness, love and hate,
Envy and anger are there.
Then would you quarrels avoid,
And peace and love rejoice?
Keep anger not only out of your words,
But keep it out of your voice.

**CUSTOMER RETENTION**

- An average business spends 6 times more to attract new customers than it does to keep existing ones.
- Customer loyalty can be worth 10 times the price of a new customer's single purchase.
- It costs 5 times as much to attract a new customer than it costs to keep an old one.
- It tacks 12 positive customer service encounters to make up for one negative incident.
- A business will hear from only 4% of it's dissatisfied customers.
- A dissatisfied will tell an average of 9 people about the problem.
- Of the 96% that don't complain, 91% will never do business with you again.
- 70% of complaining customers will give you another opportunity if you resolve the problem in their favor.
- 95% of complaining customers will give you another opportunity if you resolve the problem on the spot.

## A GOOD AND EFFECTIVE LEADER CAN:

- can create a shared vision
- makes objectives clear
- is trustworthy and fair
- gives clear goals and standards
- is consistent as well as flexible
- develops and empowers others
- offers suggestions and alternatives
- is and holds others accountable
- is available and enthusiastic
- is knowledgeable and skilled
- motivates creativity in others
- is a good listener and offers feedback
- is respectful and sensitive to everyone
- is organized and dependable
- is team orientated and delegates fairly
- gets results and follows up

- is a healthy role-model
- is a good communicator
- makes changes gradually
- gets all the facts first
- have an open-door policy

## ARE YOU LISTENING?

A recent study in the Journal of Business Communication' disclosed that good listener typically hold higher-level positions, and are promoted more often than those with less effective listening skills. The following are a few tips to help you improve during conversations.

1. During the course of the conversation, repeat the top facts in your mind so as to stay focused and be ready to use it when it is your turn to speak.
2. During a pause in the conversion, say words like, that's amazing, or unbelievable, as it will promote more interaction.
3. Try to spend at least 50% of your time listening, and don't offer to give your opinion until you feel that person has had a chance to air there views first.
4. Listen for ideas, not just facts. Listening only for facts often prevents you from grasping the persons intended meaning.
5. Avoid jumping to conclusions when someone is speaking, Don't anticipate what the they are trying to say.
6. Try to stay interested in what a person is saying even if the delivery is boring and wordy. Avoid the tendency for your mind to wander, as you have to work at listening.
7. Don't evaluate of judge how something is said. Keep listening for ideas and avoid the tendency to become upset by strong words that may bother you.

8. Never rush or interpret the speaker. Don't try and change the subject until your certain the person is done with what they had to say about a certain topic.
9. Ask questions to clarify points and to let the person know you are paying close attention.
10. Tell yourself tat the speaker is important enough to be listened to. Don't fake it.

## Only 8% Win

An international research regarding Salespeople vs. Customers was conducted in order to determine how they interacted – (known/compiled) to be the 8/73 Survey. There research revealed this:

44% gave up after the first objection
22% gave up after the second objection
16% gave up after the third objection
10% gave up after the forth objection

Therefore, 92% gave up after only four objections, leaving only 8% of salespeople still trying to sell. The 73% comes from the second part of the survey. The research determined that 73% of the customers voiced five or more initial objections before being confident enough to accept the deal. Meaning, if the 92% would have been professionally persistent, they may have closed the deal.

## Attitude is 93% of your Success

A study conducted by the Harvard Business School determined that four factors are critical to succeed in business: Information, Intelligence, Skills, and Attitude. When these factors are rated in order of importance, the first three contributed to only 7% of sales success, whereby ones' attitude contributed to a commanding 93%.

Point taken. Therefore, it seems clear that your customers are watching you closely and will pick up on negatives. Take the high road, lead by example, and close that sale!

## 10 Considerations your Clients need from a Negotiation

1. To be recognized by their boss and piers as one who possesses good judgment.
2. To meet their companies needs while maintained their budget.
3. To make their job easier and more efficient.
4. To avoid/minimize future problems and risks.
5. To feel that their decision will make a positive difference.
6. To feel good themselves and what they have to contribute is important.
7. To be thought of to be honest and fair and trustworthy.
8. To believe they made a good deal for all parties involved.
9. To feel that the final decision was theirs.
10. To know that they can count on you now and in the future.

## 7 Things your Employees Need from their Bosses

1. Know they are being treated fairly and equally.
2. Be offered ongoing training opportunities.
3. To be equally paid for doing the same job description.
4. Be given every opportunity for raises, bonus', and promotions.
5. To be given a clear direction and obtainable goals.
6. To believe their ideas are valuable and to be implemented.
7. To know they will have a positive reference when moving on.

## Attitude is Everything

Success is getting up one more time than you fall.
Doing your best is better than being the best.
If your words are soft and sweet, they won't be as hard to swallow as when you have to eat them.
Don't be afraid to admit you are wrong, it helps others feel more comfortable around you.
Appreciation is always appreciated.
The person who wins, is the person who thinks he can.
Maximum performance comes from maximum effort.
Use humor whenever you can, it's therapeutic for everyone.
When information stops, rumors start.
In order to lead by example, one must first learn self control.
You get people to do what you want not by bullying or trickery, but by understanding.
If you what to make a big difference, remember it's the little things that count.
Short term loss, long term gain. Long term loss, short term gain.
As important as the past is, it is not as important as your future can be.


## 12 Ways To Improve Your Listening Skills

1. Prepare in advance – have your questions ready to free your mind for listening.
2. Concentrate – focus on what's being said and try to shut out all distractions.
3. Don't interrupt – a pause may not mean they are finished with their point.
4. Listen for ideas – try to get the big picture of what their trying to convey.
5. Take notes – to be selective, remember points of interest, and relevance.
6. Don't argue mentally – try not to take anything personally as it can be distracting.

7. Use listening responses – try to say, "yes", or "I get that", to show comprehension
8. Use reflective phrases – try to say, "you said", or "you stated", for elaboration.
9. Limit your talking – because you can't talk and listen at the same time.
10. Think like the customer – remember, their problems are your problems.
11. Ask questions – the more you ask the more they will see you care and understand.
12. Practice listening – utilize conversations with friends and family as learning tools.

**Phraseology**

Responsible/charge of/for/to
Report directly to
Promoted to/from
Responsibilities include
Researched/developed
Established/maintained
Put into operation
Recently implemented
Successfully organized
Increased productivity/profits/sales
Put into effect/action
Hired/supervised/trained
Wrote and distributed
Managed publicity/programs
Developed new recourses /supplies
Streamlined/shortened up
Faster retrieval/ efficiency
Effected/lowered costs/savings

The following is a collection of various informative quick tips, phrases, and business principles. These can be an effective learning tool to improve your work ethic, increase your vocabulary, and enhance your level of professionalism.

Remember, the choices we make day by day shape our lives - choose how you want to live now. Like the immortal saying goes: there are three kinds of people in the world; those who make things happen, those who watch things happen, and those who say "what happened". Which one are you?

| LOSERS | WINNERS |
|---|---|
| say, I can't help it | say, if it is to be, it is to me |
| translate reality into dreams | translate dreams into reality |
| control | empower |
| say, nobody knows | say, lets find out |
| are part of the problem | are part of the solution |
| are afraid of winning | are not afraid of losing |
| are always too busy | work harder than |
| say, it was not my fault | say, I was wrong |
| have to | want to |
| often waste time | always make time |
| make promises | make commitments |
| say, I'll try to do that | say, I'll plan to do that |
| say, I'm not as bad as others | say, I'm not as good as I can be |
| wait till it's their turn to talk | listen to what others say |
| catch others doing wrong | catch others doing things right |
| resent their colleagues | learn from others |
| see only the problems | see opportunities |
| talk about it | do it |
| say I only work here | feel and act responsible |
| say, that's the way it's been | say, there ought a better way |
| complain about others | celebrate others |
| expect it on a silver platter | always expect success |
| don't know what to do | are confident of their decision |
| quit | never give up |

## SERVICE FAILURES
### SERVICE SUCCESSES

those who seem depressed or angry

those who have a positive outlook
those who would rather work alone
those who genuinely enjoy people
those who need to be the center of attention
those who put the customer on high
those who work at their own pace
those who appreciate company quota
those who are enjoy routine
those who are flexible
those who are always right
those who allow others to save face
those who are lazy and cynical
those who are willing to learn
those who aren't afraid to fail
those who learn from mistakes
those who take criticism personally
those who welcome others comments
those who are apathetic
those who listen well and care
those who leave at 5pm sharp
those who stay till the job is finished
those who waste time
those whose day just flies by
those who don't pay attention
those who remember peoples' names

**IT'S ALL IN HOW YOU SAY IT**

| INSTEAD OF SAYING: | TRY THIS: |
|---|---|
| the problem with that is | I like that |
| no way it will work | you're on the right track |
| not possible | go ahead and try it |
| it's not a bad idea but… | we can do a lot with that idea |
| we've never done it that way | that's great how do we do that |
| you haven't considered | what else do we need |
| it won't work | I think it will fly |
| it's not in the budget | lets fit it in |
| why | why not |

| | |
|---|---|
| let's do it some other time | lets do it right now |
| tomorrow | today |
| this is too tough | I enjoy a challenge |

## IF WE DON'T KNOW IT WE CAN'T SHOW IT

Legendary University football coach Paul (Bear) Bryant said, "there are five things that winning team members need to know".

1. Tell me what you can expect from me
2. Give me an opportunity to perform
3. Let me know how I'm getting along
4. Give me guidance where I need it
5. Reward me according to my contribution

## THE GREATEST

- the greatest day - "today"
- the greatest handicap - "fear"
- the greatest mistake - "giving up"
- the greatest stumbling block - "ego"
- the greatest comfort - "work well done"
- the greatest need – "common sense"
- the greatest gift – "forgiveness"

## The P's

Proper
Preparation
Prevents
Piss
Poor
Performance

## SYMTOMS OF A CLOSED MIND

- that's not my job
- we've always done it this way
- the old way, or one always worked
- our place is different
- it costs too much
- were all too busy for that
- it's too radical a change
- I tried that
- I don't have the time
- not enough help
- our organization is too small for that
- I'd like to help you, but…
- employees will never buy it
- the board will shoot it down
- we've never done it before
- it's against policy
- we don't have the authority
- I'm not sure I know how
- that's not our problem
- why change it, it's still working ok
- you're right but
- we're not ready for that
- you're two years ahead of your time
- we don't have the time, money, the equipment or the personnel
- it isn't in the budget
- can't teach an old dog new tricks
- I've never heard of that before
- good thought, but impractical
- let's give it more thought
- management would never go for it
- not that one again
- where'd you dig that one up
- we did all right without it
- it just isn't the right time
- it's never been tried before

- clients won't like it
- maybe that will work in your department but not in mine
- it can't be done
- it won't pay for itself
- I know someone who tried it
- You're never satisfied, are you?

**IT MAY BE TIME TO START THE SEARCH IF**

- you're day is getting mundane
- you're being labeled in your job description
- you're in career is not being supported
- you're buried in the minutia
- you're reputation is becoming stagnant
- you're bonus didn't get approved
- you're the only one saying thank you
- you're being confronted more frequently
- you're boss does not smile when they see you

**WHO AM I**

I am your greatest helper or your heaviest burden. I will push you onward or I will drag you down to failure. I am at your command. Half the tasks that you do, you might as well turn them over to me and I'll do them quickly and correctly. I am easily managed. You must merely be firm with me, show me exactly how you want something done and after a few lessons, I'll do it automatically. I am the servant of all great people and, alas, all failures as well. Those who are great, I have made great and those who are failures, I have made failures. I am not a machine, but I work with all precision of a machine plus the intelligence of a person. You may run me for profit or run me for ruin, makes no difference to me. Just take me, train me, and be firm with me and I'll lay the work at your feet. But you be easy with me, and I'll destroy you.
(Habit)

## ACTION WORDS

accomplished, acquired, administered, assisted, applied, affected, appraised, achieved, adapted, advised, analyzed, assertive, assisted, approved, arranged, assessed, attained, arrived, built, broadened, budgeted, catalogued, completed, concise, calculated, controlled, conceived, clarified, communicated, conceived, coached, compared, composed, conceived, constructed, controlled, constructed, controlled, contracted, convinced, correlated, directed, conducted, contributed, defined,   delegated, demonstrated, determined, created, coordinated, consolidated, counseled, contingent, designed, devised, directed, defined, disenfranchised, earned, evaluated, developed, decided, delivered, designed, directed, delegated, employed, demonstrated, designed, detailed, developed, distributed, earned, effected, enforced, encouraged, enlarged, established, estimated, equipped, evaluated, examined, executed, expanded, experimented, eliminated, equipped, established, evaluated, expanded, experience, excelled, executed, expended, formulated, exhaustive, extrapolate, expedite, fiduciary, fostered, formed, frivolous, facilitated, founded, generated, gained, governed, grouped, guided, handled, identified, improved, increased, initiated, implemented, improved, increased, influenced, illustrated, initiated, innovated, inspired, instituted, installed, interpret, integrated, interviewed, introduced, marketed, mobilized, monitored, minutia, invented, investigated, launched, lucrative, medicated, motivated, learned, led, maintained, managed, negotiated, operated, organized, obtained, organized, originated, observed, performed, persuaded, programmed, proved, provided, perceived, perhaps, participated, pioneered, prepared, presented, promoted, proposed, performed, persuaded, pertinacity, planned, processed, produced, published, recap, renovated, reported, recorded, recommended, revised, reviewed, recruited, rectified, reorganized, reviewed, postulate, reduced, reproduced, repaired, researched, saved, searched, secured, simplified, solid, solved, stimulated, strengthened, structure, succeeded, summarized, supported, sympathized, scheduled, selected, spearheaded, submitted, suggested, served, set-up, simplified, sold, streamlined, strengthened, supervised, taught, tailored, thorough, trained, transformed, treated, translated, united, validated, utilized, utopia, usurped, updated, wrote, verified, vision, worked, zapped...

## POWER/SELLING WORDS

academic, accurate, alert, administrate, bottom-line, breakthrough, congruity, competitive, concept, consistent, concise, challenge competent conscientious, dispel, dynamic, effective, expand, enterprising, edge, energetic, efficient, fundamental, flexible, formula, foothold, high-tech, intend, investigate, just do-it, launching, lively, logical, liaison, luxury, meticulous, new, notable, novel, methodical, opportunity, original, opportunity, professional, pioneer, principle, pro-active, venture, productive, proficient, panache, promising, particular, responsible reward revisit revolutionize, reliable trustworthy, thorough, supportive, successful, substantial, significant, specialized, successful, savvy, skill, technology, talent, timely  upscalevalue ultimate, variety, versatile...

## PHRASE IT RIGHT

- started as...
- in charge of...
- promoted to...
- put into effect...
- responsible for...
- reported directly to...
- responsibilities included...
- supervised a staff of over...
- researched and developed...

- established and maintained...
- effected an annual savings of...
- hired, trained and supervised...
- developed and put into operation...
- created and presented programs that...
- increased productivity – profit – sales by...
- successfully (or implemented) organized...
- lowers overhead and cost of the period of/by...
- reorganized filled system for faster retrieval and greater efficiency...
- due to my knowledge of the material, program, system, people, I was able to...
- managed publicity for..., gave talks on..., wrote and distributed press releases on ...
- saved money by: developing new sources of supplies, streamlined paper trails, and enhanced documentation, protocols, created new systems of...

# THE ONE MINUTE INTERVIEW
## CHAPTER VI

## CAREER COUNSELOR

*This Chapter is dedicated to offering both historical and current Employment Trend statistics related the Job Market and aiding you to help guide yourself in your Career. The intent here is enhance your knowledge of the options available and to provide you with valuable information to help guide yourself to the field the best suits your interests and capabilities. In this Chapter is a collection of various informative quick tips, phrases, and business principles. These can be an effective learning tool to improve your work ethic, increase your vocabulary, and enhance your level of professionalism. Remember, the choices we make day by day shape our lives - choose how you want to live now. Like the immortal saying goes: there are three kinds of people in the world; those who make things happen, those who watch things happen, and those who say "what happened". Which one are you?*

In October 2009, the unemployment rate was 10% and as of the second quarter of 2013 the unemployment rate was 7.5% with approximately 500,000 new claims per quarter), not to mention the millions of people who are searching while presently employed. The number of persons employed part time for economic reasons (sometimes referred to as involuntary part-time workers) declined by 334,000 to 7.9 million in August. These individuals were working part time because their hours had been cut back or because they were unable to find a full-time job. In August, 2013 2.3 million persons were marginally attached to the labor force, down by 219,000 in August 2012. These individuals were not in the labor force nor wanted and were available for work, and had not looked for a job sometime in the prior 12 months.

They were not counted as unemployed because they had not searched for work in the 4 weeks preceding the survey. Bottom line is: only **YOU** Truly, control your destiny!

National Unemployment Rate 5.0 Percent in September 2016 for January was 4.9% compared to August of 4.9%; 2015 January was 5.7% compared to August 5.1%; 2014 January was 6.6% and August was 6.1%; 2013 January was 7.9% and August was 7.2%

Be prepared to take a variety of "Career" and "Personality" tests during your lifetime. Whether it is part of the Interview process, or part of the process for a promotion, or simply ongoing Corporate practice. Now these have changed over the years and they all typically ask the same similar questions. Now be careful how you answer these, yea some are designed to trip you up and commit perjury yourself – so read and re-read each line carefully and do not let a time-limit rush you (that's part of their trick to trip you up!) However, be honest because if the test doesn't discover the truth, your actions down the road will. I have taken several of these and even thou the modern ones can get a scary – close synopsis of you – keep in mind human personalities in a generally fall into only a few notable categories. For me I typically and naturally fall into the middle of the road. They don't like this and is perceived as weak, non-committal, and/or dishonest, but the truth is all of change if even only slightly and can take the same test over and over and get a totally different summary each time.

Small Steps. A friend of mine started working at a McDonalds back when we were in high-school. She said that it really wasn't a bad place to work as she enjoyed working with the other employees there and enjoyed serving the customers. Even thou she was only a part-time employee she was promoted to a line level supervisor her second year there. After graduation they offer her an Assistant Managers position. Now keep in mind she always thought about going to College with some of her friends and to figure out herself and where she wanted her career to go from there. However, her parents were not necessarily well off financially and although they wanted to help pay her tuition there were not in a position to assist very much. She decided to accept the position and work it for one year so she can save up to potentially go to College the next year - which inevitably bled into two years because she bought a car. Just prior to when the 2nd year commitment was ending the Store Manager suddenly quit leaving the spot available. Yes, you guessed it, my friend was offered the position and now was in a quandary as to what to do. Fact is, now the salary was getting pretty decent, plus a bonus program, 401k and stock with salary options - plus they liked her! She thought it out, well I'm only 21 and its more money that can be saved up for College, and really what's one more year?! She ended up being the General Manager there for the next six years until they promoted her one more time to be a Regional Manager making quite a handsome salary. Could she have done better by going to College? Possibly. I lost touch with her after that but the moral of this story is don't be afraid to start at the bottom of the "totem pole", with a little hard work honesty and dedication you never know where that can lead you!

## STATS

### HISTORY OF HOW THE JOB MARKET HAS CHANGED

| The Labor Force Is Changing | 1990 | 2005 | Change |
|---|---|---|---|
| • the civilian labor force | 125 mil | 151 mil | +26% |
| The Labor Force Is a Diverse Group | | | |
| • White | 79% | 73% | -6% |
| • Black | 11% | 12% | +1% |

- Hispanic 8%
  11%         +3%
- Asian and others 3%
  4%          +1%

## Women Are Contributing To The Workforce

- Women participating in the workforce 57%
  63%         +6
- Women as a percentage in the workforce 45%
  47%         +2

## We Are No Longer A Nation Of Manufacturers, We Are A Nation Of Service Providers

- Jobs producing goods 25.0 mil
  25.2 mil    +1%
- Jobs producing services 84.4 mil
  107.4 mil   +27%

## The Labor force Is Getting Older

- Workers aged 16-24 17%
  16%         -1%
- Workers aged 25-34 29%
  21%         -8%
- Workers aged 35-54 42%
  48%         +6%
- Workers aged 55 and older 12%
  15%         +3

## The Labor Force Is More Educated

- Workers with up to 4 yrs of high school 67%
  53%         -14%
- Workers with 1 - 3 years of training 15%
  21%         +6
- Workers with 4 years of college or more 18%
  26%         +8

## FASTEST GROWING OCCUPATIONS

| OCCUPATION | GROWTH RATE |
| --- | --- |
| Occupational therapy assistants | 43% |
| Physical therapist assistants | 41% |

Physical therapist aides                         39%

Home health aides                                38%


The Largest Growing Occupations
_____

- Salespersons, retail
  3,619,000      4,506,000      24%
- Registered nurses
  1,727,000      2,494,000      44%
- Cashiers
  2,633,000      3,318,000      26%
- General office clerks
  2,737,000      3,407,000      24%
- Truck drivers
  2,362,000      2,979,000      26%
- Managers and executives
  3,086,000      3,684,000      19%
- Janitors, maids and cleaners
  3,007,000      3,562,000      18%
- Nursing aids, orderlies, attendants
  1,274,000      1,826,000      43%
- Food counter and fountain workers
  1,607,000      2,158,000      34%
- Waiters and waitresses
  1,747,000      2,196,000      26%


## HOW PEOPLE GET JOBS

                                        People Who
Tried It         Success Rate
- Applying direct to employer                66%
          48%
- Asking friends and relatives about jobs    78%
          33%

- Answering newspaper ads     46%
  24%
- Using state job service     34%
  14%
- Using private employment agency     21%
  24%
- Using school placement office     13%
  21%
- Taking civil service exam     15%
  15%
- Union hall hiring     6%
  13%

**Complete the following to help you to determine a potential Job Classification.**

Check beside the description that best suits your choices.

1. I prefer to work for company whose job openings are:
a. growing     b. stable     c. declining     d. never any changes

2. I prefer to work:
a. indoors     b. outdoors     c. indoors but no office  d. some indoor and some outdoor

3. I prefer a job that I can work:
a. a regular 8-hour day  b. irregular/flexible hours  c. night shift  d. any

4. I prefer my work environment to be:
a. laid out for me     b. lay out for others     c. some supervision     d. direct supervision

5. I prefer the job to be:
a. heavy pressure     b. no pressure   c. a mix     d. even pace

6. I prefer the job safety level to be:
a. no risk   b. a little risk   c. some risk   d. high risk

7. I prefer to travel:
a. never   b. some   c. some   d. heavy

8. I prefer the physical lifting to be:
a. under 10lbs.   b. up to 30lbs.   c. up to 50lbs   d. 50lbs and over

9. I prefer the required education level to be:
a. high school   b. undergrad   c. graduate   d. doctorate

10. I (realistically) prefer the income to be:
a. $15,000-$30,000   b. $30,000-$60,000   c. $60,000-$100,000   d. over $100,000

**The following are essay questions designed to take you from generalizing to your ultimate desired destination. Think carefully over each question, write down your thoughts then set it aside then revisit your answers from time to time.**

1. Where do you wish to live geographically?
2. Is being close to family and friends the final decision maker/ breaker?
3. Is salary your true goal to your career decision?
4. Do you prefer a routine and stable environment?
5. Have you always wanted a job that requires travel?
6. Would you rather work with lots of people?
7. Has it always been a goal to be a part of a larger Corporation?
8. Do you like to work outdoors?
9. Is being a professional with a Doctorate Degree you?
10. Is serving in a Brach of the Military fit your personality?

# THE ONE MINUTE INTERVIEW
## CHAPTER 7

### RESOURCES

The following is a collection of various names - numbers - address of various companies, web-sites, agencies, books and much more for your help and reference, but whatever you do...

**DON'T QUIT'**
When things go wrong as they sometimes will,
When the road your traveling seems all uphill,
When care is pressing you down a bit,
Rest if you must, but don't you quit.
Many a failure can turn about,
You might just win if you stuck it out,
Don't give up though the pace seems slow,
You can succeed through another blow,
So stay in the fight when your hardest hit,
When things seem worse you must not quit.
So remember this quip and you'll be known
As he who stuck it out and grown

**JOB-LINE TELEPHONE NUMBERS**

Allstate - 847 632-8527

American Association Of Nurse Anesthetists - 800 543-aana

American Medical Association - 312 464-4662

ATA - 317 240-7106

Careers in Cruise Lines - 800 929-7447

Career Vision - 216 475-2225

Coca-Cola - 317 243-3771

Conseco - 317 817-3333

Consumer Credit Counseling Service - 800 547-0099

Enterprise - 317 848-2210 x500

Free and Inexpensive Career Materials - 301 946-2553

Home Based Business - 800 350-6195 & 813 218-3495

Pep Boys - 708 681-8692

Verbal Advantage - 800 777-1987

**JOB SEARCH WEBSITES**

I have provided the following Companies Websites that you can visit for their Job-Postings:

6FigureJobs.com
Aerobic City – aerobiccity.com
ATA – ata.com
AT&T – att.com
Avis – avis.com
Boise Cascade – bcop.com
Bugetel – bugetel.com
Canon - hrchicago@cusa.canon
Carmax – carmax.com
Carson Pirie Scott & Co. – profits.com
Cellular One - c1chicago.com
Conseco - conseco.com

Dial America – dialamerica.com
Dunbar – dunbararmored.com
FedEx – fedex.com
Ford - ford.com/careercenter.com
Fujitsu Ten Corp – ftcario.com
GTE – gte.com
Harrah's Casino – hurrahs.com
Hertz – hertz.com
Hyatt – hyatt.com
Kelley Services – kelleyservices.com
Kinko's – kinkos.com
Kraft – kraftfoods.com
Manpower - manpower
Marriott - careers.marriott.com
Pep Boys – pepboys.com
Pinkerton Security – pinkertons.com
Prime Co – primeco.com
Prudential Services – prusec.com
Restaurant Career Center –restaurantcareers.com
Ryder – ryder.com
Scholarships & Fellowships - cs.cmu.edu
Sears – sears.com
7-11 - 7-eleven.com
Sheraton – Sheraton.com
Shoe Carnival – shoecarnival.com
Steak 'N Shake - steaknshake
Student Financial Aid - infi.net/collegemoney/tocl.html
Ticket Master – ticketmaster.com
Trans Union – tuc.com
U-Haul – uhaul.com
United Airlines – ual.com
United Parcel Service – ups.com
United States Trucking Driving School – ustruck.com
U.S. Freightways – usfreightways.com
USA Group – usagroup.com
Welcome Wagon International, Inc. – welcomewagon.com
Absolutely Health Care/HealthJobsUSA.com
AfterCollege.com
AgCareers.com

AllHealthcareJobs.com
AllRetailJobs.com
AmericanJobs.com
Bankingboard.com
BioSpace.com
BLACK COLLEGIAN Online
Blue Line
BrokerHunter.com
CareerBank.com
CareerBuilder.com
CareerJournal.com
Careermetasearch.com
Casino Careers Online
ccJobsOnline.com
Chronicle of Higher Education's Career Network Site
Chronicle of Philanthropy's Philanthropy Career Site
CollegeGrad.com
ComputerJobs.com
Computerwork.com
ConstructionJobs.com
ContractJobHunter.com
CoolWorks
Craigslist
CreditUnionBoard.com
dice.com
DirectEmployers.com
DiversityInc.com/careers
eFinancialCareers.com
EmploymentGuide.com
Escrowboard.com
executivetrumpet.com
Florida CareerLINK.com
GetaGovJob.com
GetTheJob.com
grantcooper.com
Great Insurance Jobs
hcareers.com
healthcareerweb.com
hotjobs.com

hoovers.com/executives
HundredkResume.com
HRJobs (SHRM.org)
IEEE Job Site
IMDiversity.com
Indeed.com
Job.com
JobCircle.com
JobFox.com
Jobing.com
JobLoft.com
JobsOnline.net
Jobscience
JobsinLogistics.com
JobsinME.com
JobsinNH.com
JobsinRI.com
jobsinthemoney.com
JobsinVT.com
Jobster.com
JournalismJobs.com
LatPro
LocalCareers.com (WisconsinJobs.com, Jobs4HR.com, Etc)
MarketingJobs.com
Math-Jobs.com
MediCenter.com
Medzilla
Military.com
MilitaryHire.com
MinnesotaJobs.com
Monster.com
Mortgageboard.com
NationJob.com
Naturejobs
netshare.com
Net-Temps
Opportunities-inc.com
PennEnergyJOBS
QUANTster.com

RecruitMilitary.com
RegionalHelpWanted.com
salary.com
ScienceCareers
SciWeb Career Center
SearchEase
Showbizjobs.com
SimplyHired.com
SnagAJob.com
SocialWorkJobBank.com
Talent Zoo
TelecomCareers.net
Telecommuting Jobs
TheLadders.com
Titleboard.com
TopBuildingJobs.com
TopUSAJobs.com
TriadCareers
TrueCareers
Vault.com
VetJobs.com
Wetfeet
Women in Technology International (WITI4Hire.com)
WorkMinistry.com
Workopolis

**HEADHUNTERS**

Manpower - 414 961-1000
Netshare - 800 241-5642
Personnel Commitment - 800 get-a-job
Search Bulletin - 800 486-9220
Smart Source - 888 tec-staff
Exec-U-Net - 800 637-3126
Spencer Stuart – 312 822 0080

## BOOKS (related)

"The One Minute Manager", by Ken Blanchard and Spencer Johnson

"The One Minute Salesman", by Larry Wilson and Spencer Johnson

"Play to Win! Choosing Growth Over Fear in Work and Life.", by Larry Wilson

"How To Have A Winning Job Interview", "How To Win The Offer", "Work At Home Jobs", by Joyce Lain Kennedy

"Joyce Lain Kennedy's Career Book"; Co-Authored by Dr. Darryl Laramore by Deborah Perlmutter Bloch; VGM Career Horizon, 4255 W. Touhy Ave. Lincolnwood, IL 60646

"How To Make $1000 A Minute: Negotiating Your Salaries And Raises" by Jack Chapman; Ten Speed Press, Box 7123 Berkeley, CA 94707

"Interview For Success: A Practical Guide To Increasing Job Interviews, Offers, And Salaries"; by Dr. Carol R. Krannich; Impact Publications, 10655 Big Oak Circle, Manassas, VA 22111

"Job-Hunt Success Tapes"; by Kent Savage and Phyllis Martin; Center for Careers Development, 7745 Reinhold Dr., Cincinnati, OH 45237

"Knock 'Em Dead With Great Answers To Tough Questions"; by Martin John Yate; Bob Adams Inc., 840 Summer St. Boston, MA 02127

"Make Then Choose You: The Executive Selection Process"; by James D. Kohlman; Corporate Advisors Inc., 250 NE 27th St. Miami, FL 33137

"Rites Of Passage At $100,000+", by John Lucht; The Viceroy Press, Box 5356, NY, NY 10185

"The Complete Q & A Interview"; By Jeffery G. Allen; John Wiley & Sons, One Wiley Dr., Somerset, NJ 08875

"The Interview Handbook": Playing to Win", by Nick Edward Nixon; American Career Publishing, Box 64980, Dallas, TX 75206

"Work At Home Jobs" Work, Box 368, Cardiff, CA 92007

"Getting the Job You Really Want", "The Very Quick Job Search", "The Right Job For You, by J. Michael Farr

"The Resume Solution", by David Swanson

"The Job Doctor", by Phillip Norris

"Work In The New Economy", by Robert Wegmann

"The Career Connection" & TCCII", by Dr. Fred Rowe

"Beyond Blue Suites and Resumes", Dr. Annette L. Segal

"Career Opportunities in Travel and Tourism", by John K. Hawks

"Making Money with Your Computer at Home" and "Finding Your Perfect Work", by Paul and Sarah Edwards

"Knock 'Em Dead" and "Beat the Odds: Career Buoyancy Tactics for Today's Turbulent Job Market", by Martin Yate

"Career Opportunities in the Music Industries", by Shelly Field

"Academic Job Search Handbook", by Mary Heiberger

"101 Great Answers to the Toughest Interview Questions", by Ron Fry

"Career Power", by Richard Koonce

"What Color Is Your Parachute", by Richard Bolles

## MISCELLANEOUS ADDRESS's

American Institute Of Certified Public Accountants
Harborside Financial center
201 Plaza III
Jersey City, NJ 07311-3881

Certified Reference Checking Guide
3466 Bridgeland Dr., Suite 200
St. Louis, MO 63044

Communication Briefings
700 Blake Horse Pike, Suite 110
Blackwood, NJ 08012 609 232-6380

The Institute Of Internal Auditors
249 Maitland Ave.
Altamonte Springs, FL 32701-4201

International Correspondence Schools
925 Oak St.
Scranton, PA 18540-9886

National Executive Housekeepers Association
1001 Eastwind Dr., Suite 301
Westerville, OH 43081 614 895-7166

# **NOTABLE QUOTABLES**

"We should all open our eyes and minds to the limitless possibilities the world has to offer", *Lisa Messenger*

"Brains and wits will beat capital spending ten times out of ten", *Ross Perot*

" Whether you think you can or whether you think you can't, you're right. *Henry Ford*

"Fanatical attention to consistency and detail", *Walt Disney*

"I want to know God's thoughts... the rest are details." *Albert Einstein*

"Leaders aren't born they are made. And they are made just like anything else, through hard work. And that's the price we'll have to pay to achieve that goal, or any goal." *Vince Lombardi*

"You were born to win, but to be a winner, you must plan to win, prepare to win, and expect to win", *Zig Ziglar*

"Humans are ambitious and rational and proud. And we don't fall in line with people who don't respect us and who we don't believe have our best interests at heart. We are willing to follow leaders, but only to the extent that we believe they call on our best, not our worst." *Rachel Maddow*

"Serve the customer above all else", *Nordstrom*

"Hard work and continuous improvement", *Eastman-Kodak*

"Honesty and integrity in all relationships", *Merck*

"An error doesn't have to become a mistake until you refuse to change it", *JFK*

"He who rows the boat is too busy to rock it", *Unknown*

"Professional Sales people have only one responsibility, and that is to make an excellent decision for their customer - and then lead him to it", *Zig Zigler*

"I'm not good? Then I'll try to be better. I have no chance? Maybe not, we'll see. I think I'm getting this. I think I'm getting this. Is it too early to go over? Let's work"
*Michael Jordan*

"If you find a job that you like, you will never have to work a day in your life"
*Unknown*

"100% of the shots you don't take don't go in". *Wayne Gretzky*

'Would you tell me, please, which way I ought to go from here?' 'That depends a good deal on where you want to get to,' said the Cat. 'I don't much care where --' said Alice. 'Then it doesn't matter which way you go,' said the Cat. '--so long as I get somewhere,' Alice added as an explanation." *Lewis Carroll, Alice's Adventures in Wonderland*

"An eye for eye only ends up making the whole world blind." *M.K. Gandhi*

"Whatever the mind can conceive and believe, the mind can achieve." *Dr. Napoleon Hill*

"Neither a lofty degree of intelligence nor imagination nor both together go to the making of genius. Love, love, love, that is the soul of genius." *Wolfgang Amadeus Mozart*

"You can have everything in life that you want if you just give enough other people what they want." *Zig Ziglar*

"Keep away from people who try to belittle your ambitions. Small people always do that, but the really great make you feel that you, too, can become great." *Mark Twain*

"Opportunity is based upon performance", *EDS*

"Management is doing things right; leadership is doing the right things." *Peter F. Drucker*

"Don't tell people how to do things, tell them what to do and let them surprise you with their results." *George S. Patton*

"Leadership is the art of getting someone else to do something you want done because he wants to do it." *Dwight Eisenhower*

"A leader is a dealer in hope." *Napoleon Bonaparte*

"Leaders shouldn't attach moral significance to their ideas: Do that, and you can't compromise." *Peter Drucker*

"I start with the premise that the function of leadership is to produce more leaders, not more followers." Ralph Nader

"Abraham Lincoln said, "once you familiarize yourself with the chains of bondage, you prepare your own limbs to wear them", *Abraham Lincoln*

"A tyrant is always stirring up some war or other, in order that the people may require a leader." Plato

"Great works are performed, not by strength, but by perseverance." *Samuel Johnson*

"I must follow the people. Am I not their leader?" *Benjamin Disraeli*

"The leadership instinct you are born with is the backbone. You develop the funny bone and the wishbone that go with it", *Elaine Agather*

"Delegating work works, provided the one delegating works, too." *Robert Half*

"Only one man in a thousand is a leader of men -the other 999 follow women." *Groucho Marx*

"The very essence of leadership is that you have to have vision. You can't blow an uncertain trumpet." *Theodore M. Hesburgh*

"The best executive is the one who has sense enough to pick good men to do what he wants done, and self-restraint to keep from meddling with them while they do it." *Theodore Roosevelt*

"The reasonable man adapts himself to the world; the unreasonable one persists in trying to adapt the world to himself. Therefore, all progress depends on the unreasonable man." *George Bernard Shaw*

"The journey is the reward." *Chinese Proverb*

"It's easy to make a buck. It's a lot tougher to make a difference." *Tom Brokaw*

"It's hard to lead a cavalry charge if you think you look funny on a horse." *Adlai Stevenson*

"Great spirits have always found violent opposition from mediocrities. The latter cannot understand it when a man does not thoughtlessly submit to hereditary prejudices but honestly and courageously uses his intelligence." *Albert Einstein*

"But the fact that some geniuses were laughed at does not imply that all who are laughed at are geniuses. They laughed at Columbus, they laughed at Fulton, they laughed at the Wright brothers. But they also laughed at Bozo the Clown." *Carl Sagan*

"You do not lead by hitting people over the head - that's assault, not leadership". *Dwight D. Eisenhower*

"Leadership can be thought of as a capacity to define oneself to others in a way that clarifies and expands a vision of the future." *Edwin H. Friedman*

"What you always do before you make a decision is consult. The best public policy is made when you are listening to people who are going to be impacted. Then, once policy is determined, you call on them to help you sell it." *Elizabeth Dole*

"In times of change, learners inherit the Earth, while the learned find themselves beautifully equipped to deal with a world that no longer exists." *Eric Hoffer*

"It is not so much that man is a herd animal, said Freud, but that he is a horde animal led by a chief." *Ernest Becker*

"I am a man of fixed and unbending principles, the first of which is to be flexible at all times." *Everett Dirksen*

"Whoever is providing leadership needs to be as fresh and thoughtful and reflective as possible to make the very best fight." *Faye Wattleton*

"Inventories can be managed, but people must be led". *Ross H. Perot*

"A community is like a ship; everyone ought to be prepared to take the helm."

"I cannot give you the formula for success, but I can give you the formula for failure: which is: Try to please everybody." *Herbert Swope*

"If I have seen farther than others, it is because I was standing on the shoulder of giants." *Isaac Newton*

"A leader must have the courage to act against an expert's advice." *James Callaghan*

"Customers want more than just products or services, they also want to be treated well" *Unknown*

"There's nothing more demoralizing than a leader who can't clearly articulate why we're doing what we're doing." *James Kouzes and Barry Posner*

"A leader or a man of action in a crisis almost always acts subconsciously and then thinks of the reasons for his action." *Jawaharlal Nehru*

"The only safe ship in a storm is leadership." *Faye Wattleton*

"Time is neutral and does not change things. With courage and initiative, leaders change things." *Jesse Jackson*

"Most important, leaders can conceive and articulate goals that lift people out of their petty preoccupations and unite them in pursuit of objectives worthy of their best efforts." *John Gardner*

"Leadership involves finding a parade and getting in front of it." *John Naisbitt*

"If your actions inspire others to dream more, learn more, do more and become more, you are a leader." *John Quincy Adams*

"The key to successful leadership today is influence, not authority." *Ken Blanchard*

"Leadership is not manifested by coercion, even against the resented. Greatness is not manifested by unlimited pragmatism, which places such a high premium on the end justifying any means and any measures." *Margaret Chase Smith*

"When leaders take back power, when they act as heroes and saviors, they end up exhausted, overwhelmed, and deeply stressed." *Margaret J. Wheatley*

"it isn't enough to simply perform the duties of your job, you must also have the right approach". Unknown

"The manager asks how and when; the leader asks what and why." *Warren Bennis*

"I suppose leadership at one time meant muscles; but today it means getting along with people. *M. K. Gandhi*

"It is the responsibility of intellectuals to speak the truth and expose lies." *Noam Chomsky*

"What is the managers job? It is to direct the resources and the efforts of the business toward opportunities for economically significant results. This sounds trite -- and it is. But every analysis of actual allocation of resources and efforts in business that I have ever seen or made showed clearly that the bulk of time, work, attention, and money first goes to problems rather than to opportunities, and, secondly, to areas where even extraordinarily successful performance will have minimal impact on results. The leaders who work most effectively, it seems to me, never say "I." And that's not because they have trained themselves not to say "I." They don't think "I." They think "we"; they think "team." They understand their job to be to make the team function. They accept responsibility and don't sidestep it, but "we" gets the credit. This is what creates trust, what enables you to get the task done. *Peter Drucker*"

"Systems thinking is a discipline for seeing wholes. It is a framework for seeing interrelationships rather than things, for seeing patterns of change rather than static "snapshots." It is a set of general principles -- distilled over the course of the twentieth century, spanning fields as diverse as the physical and social sciences, engineering, and management.... During the last thirty years, these tools have been applied to understand a wide range of corporate, urban, regional, economic, political, ecological, and even psychological systems. And systems thinking is a sensibility -- for the subtle interconnectedness that gives living systems their unique character." *Peter Senge*

"Abraham Lincoln did not go to Gettysburg having commissioned a poll to find out what would sell in Gettysburg. There were no people with percentages for him, cautioning him about this group or that group or what they found in exit polls a year earlier. When will we have the courage of Lincoln?" *Robert Coles*

"Good leaders must first become good servants." *Robert Greenleaf*

"Keep your fears to yourself, but share your inspiration with others." *Robert L. Stevenson*

"Leaders are more powerful role models when they learn than when they teach." *Rosabeth M. Kantor*

"Leaders takes people where they want to go. A great leader takes people where they don't necessarily want to go, but ought to be." *Rosalynn Carter*

"Effective leadership is putting first things first. Effective management is discipline, carrying it out." *Stephen Covey*

"Cautious, careful people, always casting about to preserve their reputation and social standing, never can bring about a reform. Those who are really in earnest must be willing to be anything or nothing in the world's estimation, and publicly and privately, in season and out, avow their sympathy with despised and persecuted ideas and their advocates, and bear the consequences." *Susan B. Anthony*

"The very essence of leadership is that you have to have a vision." *Theodore Hesburgh*

"If you're not confused, you're not paying attention." *Tom Peters*

"The art of leadership is saying no, not yes. It is very easy to say yes." *Tony Blair*

"Some leaders are born women." *unknown*

"The final test of a leader is that he leaves behind him in other men the conviction and the will to carry on." *Walter Lippman*

"South African Archbishop Desmond Tutu walked by a construction site on a temporary sidewalk the width of one person. A white man appeared at the other end, recognized Tutu, and said, "I don't make way for gorillas." At which Tutu stepped aside, made a deep sweeping gesture, and said, "Ah, yes, but I do." *Walter Wink*

"The most dangerous leadership myth is that leaders are born -- that there is a genetic factor to leadership. This myth asserts that people simply either have certain charismatic qualities or not. That's nonsense; in fact, the opposite is true. Leaders are made rather than born." *Warren G. Bennis*

"The price of greatness is responsibility." *Winston Churchill*

"Leadership and learning are indispensable to each other." *John F. Kennedy*

"A good leader inspires others with confidence in him; a great leader inspires them with confidence in themselves." *Unknown*

"A good leader can't get too far ahead of his followers." *Franklin D. Roosevelt*

"Forethought and prudence are the proper qualities of a leader." *Tacitus*

"Leadership is getting someone to do what they don't want to do, to achieve what they want to achieve." *Tom Landry*

"Good leaders develop through a never-ending process of self-study, education, training, and experience." *From the 'Manual on Military Leadership'*

"He who cannot agree with his enemies is controlled by them." *Chinese proverb*

"Leadership is action, not position." *Donald H. McGannon*

"There are many elements to a campaign leadership is number one. Everything else is number two." *Bernd Brecher*

"A good leader is not the person who does things right, but the person who finds the right things to do." *Anthony T. Dadovano*

"I am more afraid of an army of 100 sheep led by a lion than an army of 100 lions led by a sheep." *Talleyrand*

"The final test of a leader is that he leaves behind him in other men the conviction and the will to carry on." *Walter Lippmann*

"Great necessities call forth great leaders." *Abigail Adams*

"Leaders don't force people to follow—they invite them on a journey." *Charles S. Lauer*

"Children need love especially when they don't deserve it." *Harold S. Hulbert*

"I start with the premise that the function of leadership is to produce more leaders, not more followers." *Ralph Nader*

"Leadership has a harder job to do than just choose sides. It must bring sides together." *Jesse Jackson*

"I have to get the most energy out of a man and have discovered that it cannot be done if he hates another man. Hate blocks his energy and he isn't up to par until he eliminates it and develops a friendly feeling... (towards all his teammates.)" *Knute Rockne*

"The first step to leadership is servant hood." *John Maxwell*

"The first responsibility of a leader is to define reality." *Max DePree*

"If you have trouble meeting people, pick up someone else's golf ball", *Jack Lemmon*

"When you tell the truth, you only have to remember half of what you say".
*Abraham Lincoln*

"I never had much faith in leaders. I am willing to be charged with almost anything, rather than to be charged with being a leader. I am suspicious of leaders, and especially of the intellectual variety. Give me the rank and file every day in the week. If you go to the city of Washington, and you examine the pages of the Congressional Directory, you will find that almost all of those corporation lawyers and cowardly politicians, members of Congress, and mis-representatives of the masses -- you will find that almost all of them claim, in glowing terms, that they have risen from the ranks to places of eminence and distinction. I am very glad I cannot make that claim for myself. I would be ashamed to admit that I had risen from the ranks. When I rise, it will be with the ranks, and not from the ranks." *Eugene V. Beds*

"Your supervisor doesn't have to make sense. While at work be sure to do your very best, and leave it there, don't let work problems be the focus as there are other things in life that are of more important and of lasting value." *Richard Ciavarelli*

## I Hope This Helps!

**OFFICIAL COPYRIGHT REGISTRATION NUMBER TXu1-152-307**

# WORK SEARCH LOG

Company Name _____
Contact Name _____
Address _____
_____
Zip _____ Fax # _____
Phone # _____ Ext # _____

Job Title _____
Job Description _____
_____

Referred By _____
First Contact Date _____ / _____
Resume & Cover _____ [ ] yes ____ [ ] not required _____
Submitted References _____ [ ] yes ____ [ ] not required _____
Completed Application _____ [ ] yes ____ [ ] not required _____
Follow-up Letter _____ [ ] yes ____ [ ] not required _____
Additional Call Dates _____ / _____ / _____
Additional Interviews _____ [ ] yes ____ [ ] not required _____
Acceptance Letter _____ [ ] yes ____ [ ] not required _____

Interview Recap _____
_____
_____

Possible Improvements _____
_____
_____

Important Names & Titles _____
_____
_____

Important Facts _____
_____
_____

Location _____
Travel Time _____ Distance _____

© Copyright 1995 CBOA TXu 671-066

www.ingramcontent.com/pod-product-compliance
Lightning Source LLC
Chambersburg PA
CBHW060401190526
45169CB00002B/695